CLAUDIA AZULA A[...]

WSJ BESTSELLING CO-AUTHOR OF *THE POWER OF NO*

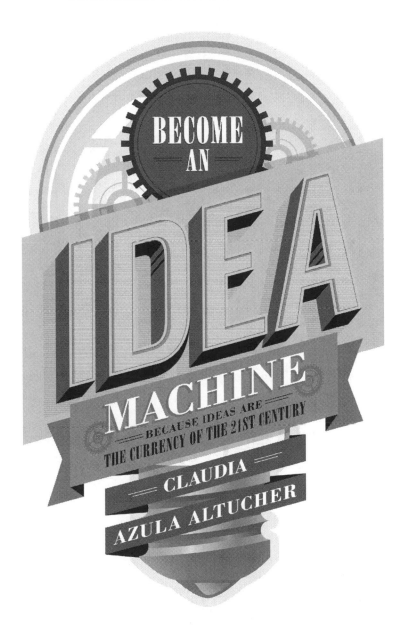

BECOME AN IDEA MACHINE

BECAUSE IDEAS ARE THE CURRENCY OF THE 21ST CENTURY

CLAUDIA AZULA ALTUCHER

ISBN-13: 978-1502593009 • ISBN-10: 1502593009

BECOME AN IDEA MACHINE

BECAUSE IDEAS ARE THE CURRENCY OF THE 21ST CENTURY

Copyright © Claudia Azula Altucher

First Edition: January 2015

ISBN-13: 978-1502593009

ISBN-10: 1502593009

Cover Design And layout: Erin Tyler

CHOOSE YOURSELF
MEDIA LLC.

DEDICATION

To all who may be struggling, stuck, feeling pressure or fear.

*May the prompts on these pages fill your days with new
ways of looking at the world.*

May your passions be ignited, your creativity soar.

*May your life, and that of those around you become magical,
abundant, and filled with bright ideas.*

May you become idea-wealthy and a magnet for success.

TABLE OF CONTENTS

FOREWORD:
BY JAMES ALTUCHER

The way to have good ideas is to get close to killing yourself. It's like weightlifting. When you lift slightly more than you can handle, you get stronger. In life, when the gun is to your head, you either figure it out, or you die. When you cut yourself open, you bleed ideas. If you're broke and close to death, you have to start coming up with ideas. If you destroy your life, you need to come up with ideas to rebuild it.

The only time I've been FORCED to have good ideas is when I was up against the wall. My life insurance policy was like a gun to my head: "Come up with good ideas... OR ELSE your kids get your life insurance!" Or at an airport when I realized a business I had been working on for four years was worthless. Or when I was getting a divorce and I was lonely and afraid I wouldn't make any money again or I wouldn't meet anyone again. Or my kids would hate me. Or I would disgust my friends.

The problem is this: you're NOT in a state of panic most of the time. States of panic are special and have to be revered. Think about the times in your life that you remember – it's exactly those moments when you hit bottom and were forced to come up with ideas, to get stronger, to connect with some inner force inside you with the outer force.

This is why it's important NOW to strengthen that connection to that idea force inside of you. This book is about HOW.

Nothing you ever thought of before amounted to anything – that's why you are exactly where you are at that moment of hitting bottom. Because all of your billions of thoughts have led you to right there. You can't trust the old style of thinking anymore. They came, they saw, they lost. You have to come up with a new way of thinking. A new way of having ideas. A new ways of interacting with the outside universe.

People know what "runner's high" is. It's when you are running for a long time, at the point of exhaustion, and then something kicks in and gives you a "second wind". 400,000 years ago people didn't jog for exercise. They didn't even have jogging shorts. Or sneakers. 400,000 years ago people need to eat and live. And either you're running to catch a prey, or you are running from a lion. You're the prey! And you need that second wind in both cases or you DIE.

The same thing happens in the brain. When you are about to die, a second wind kicks in. Ideas, experiences, opportunity, and probably hidden forces and neurochemicals we don't understand. But you can't get runners' high unless you're ALREADY in good shape. It's not possible unless you are already able to run long distances. This is why it's important to exercise the idea muscle right now. If your idea muscle atrophies, then even at your lowest point you won't have any ideas. How long does it take this muscle to atrophy? The same as any other muscle in your body: just two weeks without having any ideas. Atrophied. If you lie down in a bed for two weeks and don't move your legs you will need physical therapy to walk again.

Many people need idea therapy. Not so that they can come up with great ideas right this second (although maybe you will) but so that people can come up with ideas when they need them: when their car is stuck, when their house blows up, when they are fired from their job, when their spouse betrays them, when they go bankrupt or lose a big customer, or lose a client, or go out of business, or get sick.

IDEAS ARE THE CURRENCY OF LIFE. Not money. Money gets depleted until you go broke. But good ideas buy you good experiences, buy you better ideas, buy you better experiences, buy you more time, save your life. Financial wealth is a side effect of the "runner's high" of your idea muscle. Whoa! That was a big intro.

Sometimes people ask, "Did you only start coming up with ideas because you already had it made?"

No, I was on the floor crying because I was dead broke and dead lonely and had no prospects so that's why I had to do it.

What do I mean by an idea machine?

You will be like a superhero. It's almost a guaranteed membership in the Justice League of America. Every situation you are in, you will have a ton of ideas. Any question you are asked, you will know the response. Every meeting you are at, you will take the meeting so far out of the box you'll be on another planet, if you are stuck on a desert highway – you will figure the way out, if you need to make money you'll come up with 50 ideas to make money, and so on.

After I started exercising the idea muscle, it was like a magic power had unleashed inside of me. It's ok if you don't believe me. Or maybe you think it's bragging. There are many times when I don't have ideas. But that's when I stop practicing what I am about to advocate.

Try it for yourself. I have no reason for you to try this. I just want to share my experience. Its like part of your brain is opened up and a constant flow of stuff, both good and bad, gets dropped in there. From where? I don't think about it and I don't care. But I use it.

In early 2009 was one of those times when I desperately needed to do this. I was fulltime either trying to find a girlfriend or I was trying to start a business or both. I was also going broke in the stock market and losing my home.

Every night, I'd have waffles for dinner and a bottle of wine and start writing ideas down. This is before I went paleo (no waffles!) and stopped drinking alcohol (five years sober!) and I was writing 10-20 of the most ludicrous ideas a day down. And you know what? It worked.

BECOME AN IDEA MACHINE
IN 180 DAYS

I was laid off from my corporate 'safe' job in March of 2009. After ten years of service I got nothing.

At first it hurt like hell. And it wasn't just me; many of my friends were laid off at that time, and I only see that trend continuing. Open any newspaper and you will see who is out of a job today. There is no denying that things have changed. The entire economy has turned upside down. Everyone I know has been fired or demoted.

I don't need a Harvard study to prove that we all want *passive,* or any form of income, and enough cash in the bank so we don't obsess over where the next meal will come from. None of us want our livelihoods to depend on a boss or someone giving us commands all day.

We want freedom because we sense that we were not meant for the cubicle and the annual reviews. That is not how we spent the first thousands of years in this planet.

But when we are broke the mind tends to control us, and if we don't watch out it starts to run the show with all sorts of dead-end, scary, and never-ending "what ifs" type of scenarios where we always end up in misery.

There is a way out of it, so instead of our thoughts controlling us and flushing our life through some thought diarrhea toilets, we can train it to work *for* us, and to move us in the direction of a life of fulfillment. One day at a time.

The way is this: come up with ten ideas a day.

That's it.

When we come up with ideas every day, the repercussions are not just that we might get a better technique for a negotiation or an idea for a new company or a new way of looking at a problem.

Coming up with ten ideas a day is like exercise. And exercise makes the idea muscle stronger.

Writing daily ideas is effective because when we practice making our brain *sweat,* consistently, we become *idea machines.* When we are idea machines problems get solutions and questions get answers. We all know that lucks favor the prepared mind. I have found that the key to luck is developing the idea muscle and becoming an idea machine.

When you come up with 10 ideas a day, or about 3000 ideas a year (depending on weather you include weekends or not), ideas will explode out of you. You will be unstoppable in every situation. And the reason why is we begin to trust the words that come out of our mouths because our mind muscle has had its workout. What we say is backed by thousands of ideas that have been churned around in our mind. We have the gift of trained spontaneity.

And to become an idea machine, the tool you are holding in your hand is the way. This book is the key to getting your idea muscle in perfect shape.

Many listen, but not all do the work that is required to be extraordinary and to put in the effort required. And you will be able to tell. You might start this journal with fervor, filled with excitement, only to then find it lost under a couch six months later with only the first three days filled in.

That's OK. I have experienced this many times, not just with daily idea generation practice but also with my yoga, breathing, and meditation practices. They all take time. Only the level of ardor we feel for transformation will dictate how soon we commit and therefore how soon we get our rewards. When we see that the idea machine practice works, then it is difficult to go back.

I cannot vouch for how it will work for you, but I can tell you how it went for me.

When I first heard James talk about the idea generation part of the daily practice I liked it, but I was hesitant.

Coming from a yoga background where the goal is *the cessation of the chattering mind,* I thought this might reinforce my thinking, get me deeper into the loop of my own thoughts, and make it harder to concentrate.

Also, I was lazy; I didn't want to come up with ten ideas a day. It felt like a drag.

In 2011 when he started speaking seriously about the four legs of the daily practice on his first self-published book, I got sick and spent about six months mostly in bed, which meant he was 180 days worth of daily-ideas ahead of me.

During my lethargic state I saw James's life transform in front of my own eyes. By the time I healed he had three self-published books and was working on a fourth one, which was *professionally* self-published, something new that nobody had heard of before. It was a book done "the right way", and it was called *Choose Yourself.*

He got involved in businesses worth billions of dollars. He watched as his investments came through, often with his help and because of his idea, and to great abundance.

Re-building my yoga practice after being bed-ridden was a huge challenge. I couldn't believe how my muscles that had been so strong and supple pre-Lyme were now so stiff. My stamina was low, and my concentration was nowhere to be found.

But together with the recovery of my yoga practice I reluctantly started writing ideas every day as well, because seeing James was irrefutable proof to me that the idea muscle is real and that it works.

It sounds funny to say that ideas are a "muscle". And it may sound like it is medically incorrect. However, I would argue it is a muscle within one of the many bodies we have. We have a physical, a spiritual, an emotional and a mental body. The idea muscle is what powers the later.

As my yoga practice continued to come back I discovered something even more fascinating. Yes yoga is a road towards silencing the monkey mind. But I haven't yet found the "off" switch. Whenever my mind starts going it just does, and it has a lot to say.

But, writing ideas every day gave me a way to channel the energy that is already there. It's like a training tool for the monkey.

Whenever I feel the verbal diarrhea start to pour I tell my mind: I see that you are active, let's come up with ideas now. Let's use this energy for something positive rather than continue this exhausting loop of blaming and complaining that keeps on draining me.

Remember: complaining is draining. So I wanted to make better use of that energy rather than fight it.

In coming up with ideas every day I found a way to actually become more concentrated, because by the time my mind had worked hard at coming up with more than two or three ideas, and had to sweat all the way to ten, then it was a bit tired, and sitting in silence became more accessible, more peaceful and more effective.

Choose Yourself went on to sell hundreds of thousands of copies and influence and change lots of lives, including my own.

EVER SINCE INCORPORATING THE IDEA MUSCLE OF THE DAILY PRACTICE, I HAVE:

- Written three books,
- Lead yoga retreats and classes (something I was scared of doing before)
- Made dozens of yoga YouTube videos in English and Spanish
- Designed a yoga routine for busy people called Portable Yoga

- Started my own yoga podcast: The Yoga Podcast (dot com).
- Began co-hosting the "Ask Altucher" show with James
- Became a WSJ and USA Today best-selling author.

I am not saying this to boast, this is just the natural result of becoming an *idea machine*, and although it feels good to say, it was work!

Starting with coming up with the ideas, every single day, until one resonated so much that I just HAD to stand up and go do the first thing so that it would happen.

None of that materialized overnight. For me it took more than 180 days, it took a year, and I will tell you why, because in the beginning I was doing the idealist once or twice a week.

The *daily* practice of listing 10 ideas a day started six months ago, and by the time this book is published I will probably have several guests in my yoga podcast and maybe another book in the works, or... who knows? Ideas get unpredictable, and fun! All I know is that every six months life changes in totally unpredictable, magical ways when I exercise this muscle.

But you should not believe a word I say. However, you could try it and see what happens for you.

Yesterday I was sitting in front of Tony Robbins. We were in his house in Florida and James was interviewing him for his podcast. I was the tech girl and groupie. Well, mostly just the groupie.

Hearing Tony was transformational, he is more than an idea machine. He is what I call an *atomic idea machine*, someone that is beyond the 10 a day.

At one point he said that his intention is to help as many people as he can. And the first thing he wants to do is clarify things. For example, he wants people who make, say 30,000 dollars a year, to understand that they are not poor. In fact, they ARE the 1% they complain about.

As of January of 2013 almost half the world lived on less than $2.5 a day, and

80% of the world lived on less than $10 a day.[1] When seeing it that way I get very humbled because I realize I am one of the few that get to eat today.

We can play victim, we can be enraged, we can get angry, or we can take responsibility and decide that there is a way to change our faith.

And change can only start with us. From within by making sure we are physically healthy (take a walk, bathe, take care of your health), mentally healthy (practicing the ideas of this book), spiritually healthy by going beyond "thank you" and really feeling gratitude for new and different things every day, and emotionally healthy by surrounding ourselves with people that support and cheer us up.

If you do practice the 180 exercises in this book your mind will start to operate from a different place, because within a few weeks, or even days, it will become trained in delivering that extra bit of energy that is required whenever we need to come up with more than 3 things to say…

For example: if someone asked me to come up with one idea to improve Jet Blue (my favorite airline) I'd say: Sure! If someone asked for *two* ideas, then, hm, yeah, OK, I can come up with a second. *Three*? OK, yes, let me think… Here it is. That much is easy.

But *four* ideas!

Five? … Ten?!!!

Now we are in a different realm, we've entered the universe that is inhabited only by people who dare go into unknown territory.

By the fourth idea we've joined the non-complainers, those brave enough to face the huge waves that take you from "what ifs" to "I can do this", and surf them safely to shore, with all 10 ideas in hand.

Every time Jet Blue sends me a feedback form I know exactly what to say, how to say it, and when to send it so that they will listen. Do they? I don't know

---

1 This is the page where I found these sources http://www.globalissues.org/article/26/poverty-facts-and-stats

and I don't care, I give away all my good ideas in a useful way, and for free.

Once an idea machine, it is in giving them away that we get to add value to others with no expectation in return.

And when we add value abundance comes back like a boomerang.

The mental side of the daily practice is only one of the legs. There are three others, of course, and in each page you will have a box to check on the other three legs, to make sure you are paying attention to all of them.

If you practice, your life will transform for the better, magical things will begin to happen, and you will find yourself in the right place at the right time.

Every six months. That is the promise.

There is no other evolutionary choice.

IDEAS ARE THE
NEW CURRENCY

Not only will ideas help you co-create a transformative life that will change every six months, it will also attract abundance into your life, of every kind, not just money, but people, connections, creativity, good relationships, and peace.

When James first said that: "ideas are the new currency" it hit me like a million bricks. He had just had a massive universal download. Of course! I thought. That is a universal truth.

How do I know this is true?

When Yahoo! offered to buy Facebook for a billion dollars in 2006, billion-aire Peter Thiel called in a board meeting.

As Mark Zuckerberg entered the room he said:

"Okay, guys, this is just a formality, it shouldn't take more than 10 minutes. We're obviously not going to sell".

That is how Thiel recalls the scene[2].

And I think that meeting should have been in the movie (The Social Network) but it wasn't, and yet, it is a critical piece of history. It is key because Mark knew that he had a vision that Yahoo could not possibly have.

At 22 he was *idea-wealthy.* He was an idea machine, and beyond. Even if Facebook sold that day (and he would have made 250,000 million dollars) he would, and I paraphrase: *"probably just build another social network, although he*

---

2   Listen to James' podcast with Thiel to hear the story from the man himself. http://askaltucher.com/thiel/

liked the one he already had".

Money didn't matter much. Money was put in perspective. It was a side effect. He wanted to keep his company because he enjoyed it. But no matter what, he had so many ideas he was unstoppable.

When we look at the questions we get on AskAltucher.com (which I co-host), or, on James's Twitter Q&A's every Thursday, by far the majority have to do with the mental side of the daily practice.

Some people get confused (Is a 'to-do' a valid list of ideas? No!), some people would like suggestions, a place where to start. That is why this book is unique, because it is the tip of the iceberg on your journey of transformation by becoming an idea machine.

Within six to eight months of practicing the suggestions here (maybe you do them 7 days a week or maybe 5 times a week depending on how badly you want it), if you play fair, you will be as wealthy as the Facebook CEO was when he entered that meeting in 2006.

If you practice and make your idea muscle sweat and get in good shape, then 250 million dollars will not even mean that much, because idea generation, of the good kind, the kind that helps you AND OTHERS, which is the type you will exercise in this book, is worth ten times that, or more.

So, there is nothing to lose in trying. Take a snapshot of your life today and then revisit exactly the day you finish the book. *Mark* it in your calendar, pun intended. Feel the magic for yourself.

Not only is this book unique, it is also useful, because it may happen that one day, the suggestion I pose for your list sounds horrible. Maybe they ask you to list things related to something you know nothing about, or they ask you to come up with ideas that you don't care for.

That's OK. However, as an idea-machine, you know full well that it is your responsibility to come up with 10 ideas of your own. Because who is to say? Maybe you wake up with ideas already floating in your head. So go ahead, *you* can define your own list of ideas - We are all about choosing ourselves after all.

But, you must make sure that your brain *sweats* as much as it would if you were to follow the original idea.

Every time I do the exercise of coming up with ideas I come to a wall. It usually happens at around idea #4 or #7. There is a moment there where my mind goes: "Oh! Forget this! I hate it".

We all go through that moment. I call it the "idea freak out moment". But this is also the vortex on which we have the option to turn pro. It is where we own our idea machine power.

Only the brave ones cross it by admitting that they feel it, and in spite of it, finish the job.

On any day, past idea #5, your brain is sweating mental sweat. And that is what distinguishes you from any other person who happens to think of something. You are focusing your mind and making it work, you are fine-tuning it; you are turning it into an asset.

When you do change your ideas, make sure that your list is super specific. It is not enough to list 10 movies you liked, you need to come up with the 10 scenes you loved within the 10 movies you liked and why, and then think of a different way in which you would have delivered the punch line. Challenge yourself! Give your mind a workout.

The ideas you will find here will make you get down to the very essence of what life is made of. It is by sweating on these pages that you find value for TODAY, for you and for others.

You may come up with some pretty silly ideas along the way. But there is NEVER a bad idea. All ideas are just ideas. Write and flow with them.

Some days will be better than others, you can be sure of that. As long as you make the brain sweat a little then let it roam, let it flow, let it dream…

Some days you will be challenged to come up with *idea sex*, meaning that you will take ideas from a previous day, and combine with them with the ideas from another day. But do not worry, by the time the first idea-sex exercise pops up you will be already pretty warmed up. And you will figure it out. Because you can.

Don't even get me started on how you have no time to do the ideas "one day". Don't. Just don't. There is always a train ride or a car ride or the moment you are in the bathroom, or the shower (keep a pad next to the shower – you *must* write them down). In fact, there is a list that has you looking for this time, within your day: 10 moments. You know you have them.

Your brain is like a rocket. It requires a lot of fuzz and fuel and thinking and engineering and mental power to get started, and then even more to take off, but once it breaks free from the atmosphere it just goes smoothly into the outer space of infinite possibilities.

Yes it will be hard the first three, four, or even twelve weeks. But at some point you will feel it. There will be a lift, a propelling momentum that is unmistakably the sign of an idea muscle that has reached the stratosphere. Congratulations: You are an idea machine.

I wrote this book in six weeks. And I credit that to the idea muscle. I can only hope it is as toned as my yoga flow from downward to upward dog.

EXECUTION IS A
SUBSET OF IDEAS

S ome people in Twitter defied me and told me that ideas without execution
are nothing.

However, after listing my 10 ideas on the subject I realized that there could be
no execution over nothing. The idea has to come first. Idea precedes execution.

Or, as James will happily tell you (he always sees things differently than me),
"execution is a subset of ideas".

Further, you may have thousands of ideas, but when one of them is good,
you *feel* it. It takes over you like sunshine on the beach. It overwhelms you with
light. That is what happened to me when I had the idea to write this book.

It's as if the idea came from somewhere else. It was not mine. It was a result
of the practice of listing things. I had done the work for the muscle to be in shape
and then the "download" or the "inspiration" hit me. My heart and head went on
fire. I HAD to sit down and start writing.

Did I care that this was James idea first? NO! Did I care what people would
think? Absolutely no! Take for example what Daniel said to me in a comment
in Quora:

*"Yesterday I wrote about 20 Ideas. And the last one is my absolute favorite. I
also implemented some of the ideas already. And it gives me the feeling, that the day
wasn't wasted."*

A comment like that feels like a reward. Someone was inspired because of
my ideas. The fire keeps on igniting, and it lights up others. But that is because I
did the work first.

The muse, or the inspiration, does not just show up, it requires sweat as an offering.

And when the idea *hit* me I HAD to do it, there was no option, it just felt right, I stood up from the sofa and went to the computer as if driven by a force I knew not of before.

James said something and I answered: "sorry honey I need to go write something". Six hours later he came looking for me. I forgot to eat.

That is what happens when you train your idea muscle and then you stumble on one you love. You are acting from inspiration, there are no goals, there is just flow, there is just now, and this amazing feeling of doing something really good.

So go ahead and start with the first list suggestion on the book. It does not matter when you start it. It can be January 1st or May 2nd or September 23rd or December 14th.

Who cares?

No, really, I am asking you: Who cares? Who is the voice in your head telling you there has to be a "right day". Talk to that voice and tell it you are now choosing yourself. Come up with ten ideas as of why it really does not matter. Go idea machine on your doubts.

And write to me please, I would be grateful if you share your transformations. Because I know only good things are coming for you. And I want to be a witness.

FREQUENTLY ASKED
QUESTIONS

IS THERE A METHOD TO THE IDEA-LIST IN THE BOOK?

Yes, you will notice that the first batch of lists will benefit you, meaning that the ideas are designed with the focus on how you can improve your own life. That will go on for the first 90 days. After that you will be well on the way, with your idea machine in good shape and fired up, so we will start to focus on coming up with ideas for others.

When the ideas you generate are good the important thing is to give them away and to give them for free, or, as "currency" meaning you are paying it forward, with no expectations, and then you just watch the boomerang effect bring abundance into your own life.

SHOULD I GO IN ORDER?

Yes.

IS A TO DO LIST A VALID IDEA LIST?

No. To do lists add anxiety to our lives. Look at the example on the day where you will be listing your "I did" list.

WHAT IF I CAN'T COME UP WITH TEN?

Then come up with 20. Chances are you are suffering from a perfectionist attack. Coming up with 20 will force you to have some bad ideas, and it will loosen up the process.

Is "The Idea Muscle", or the Mental side of the daily practice, the most important part of the four?

No. They are all equally important. If you get sick, then you can't be as creative. That is why you will see at the end of each day a check-box for the other three legs of the daily practice, physical, spiritual and emotional.

My idea muscle has atrophied. How long will it take to become an idea machine?

If you come up with 10 ideas a day for 180 days it's likely, based on what both James and I have observed from 1000's of others then you will be a full force idea machine.

I have so many ideas, I don't know which ones to work on? How do you pick?

Don't. I never pick an idea. But ideas do choose me, that is why you are reading this now, it's because the idea chose me with the force of a tornado and moved me from a couch to a computer and had me typing this book. When an idea has electricity in it you will have no choice but to move into action. And you will love it because it will set your heart on fire.

What is Idea sex?

All of life is about connecting the dots. Life on Earth is about organic molecules combining and creating something new.

I once did an experiment during a workshop. I asked attendees to write down 10 titles of books they would like to write. Then choose a partner and make a list of ten books combining the titles.

There were fascinating results. For instance: "How to Make Toast in Space" or "A History of Music as Told by the Instruments of the greatest performers". Idea sex is mixing ideas and releasing control. It might lead to the birth of brilliant, more powerful ideas.

PEOPLE SAY IDEAS ARE A DIME A DOZEN AND THAT EXECUTION IS EVERYTHING. IS THIS TRUE?

No. Ideas are a dime for 3. A dozen ideas are hard. Try it, you will see.

ARE THE IDEAS USUALLY ABOUT STARTING NEW BUSINESSES?

No, usually not. It's really hard to come up with 3,650 business ideas a year. Money is just a side effect of being an idea machine.

I KEEP COMING UP WITH GOOD IDEAS BUT THEN I GO OUT DRINKING WITH MY FRIENDS ON FRIDAY NIGHT AND TELL THEM MY IDEAS AND THEY ALL LAUGH AT ME. WHAT SHOULD I DO?

Stay home on Friday night.

I'VE BEEN DOING THIS FOR THREE MONTHS AND I HAVEN'T SEEN ANY DIFFERENCE IN MY LIFE?

Do it for three more months and you will. Every day.

I HAVE NO TIME TO DO THIS. WHAT SHOULD I DO?

Make a list of the 10 ways you waste time every day.

I HAVE AN IDEA. HOW DO I GET MONEY FOR IT?

You don't. You have to implement it. You have to have other people who like it. You have to get money from customers who like it.

Go old school. Deliver proven value to others, get testimonials about how good your product is, and then you've widened the horizon of your decisions. That's the path to success.

WHAT IF I HAVE MORE THAN 10 IDEAS A DAY? SHOULD I SAVE SOME OF THEM FOR THE NEXT DAY?

No, write them all down. Let your idea machine show you what is capable of. Let the inspiration flow. You will become so solid in your ideas you will never fear things again, because you will always come up with exciting, different, out-of-the-box solutions.

Is there a level beyond
Idea-Machine?

Yes, there are two levels that I have identified.

About a month ago I listened to the podcast that James had with Noah Kagan. I laughed, I felt embarrassed, my jaw dropped a couple of times, and I was impressed.

James and Noah together kept coming up with an idea a minute. Just like comedians usually have to come up with a joke per minute, well they did the same, with ideas. It is humbling to listen.

That podcast made me notice that both James and Noah were years ahead of me. They were beyond idea machines… they were in a different level.

I call that "*Idea Atomic Machine*".

You will recognize an atomic idea machine easily, because if you ask them a question they will probably answer you with, not one, but hundreds of suggestions, and 90% of them will be excellent, so when you encounter one of them in your life you better have a tape recorder or a pen and paper ready, and write fast.

Just to illustrate, after that podcast I emailed Noah and he gave me a suggestion to create a class, and put it on Eventbrite. He also held me accountable, he asked me "when" was I going to have everything ready (including a paypal account). I was hesitant, but I felt I had to respond, so I said Thursday, giving myself a mere 48 hours.

He responded and said he would check on me by Friday. The nerve! But it was the best thing that could happen to me. Through that process I learned that I could do it and I created a wonderful two-hour workshop on yoga for back pain prevention which I will be repeating often. Such is the power of encountering an atomic-idea machine in your life.

As life kept moving I also met a chemistry genius that James works with. And just like that I realized there is even a level beyond the atomic-idea machine…

I call it the "*Super Nova Idea Machine*".

The *super nova idea machine* not only is an atomic idea machine, but every one of his or her ideas can and will change the world for the better.

Their ideas are all in service of others, and again, 90% of them are great. This guy in particular is coming up with ideas to producing energy by leveraging the morning traffic, and others that sound way too out there for me to even mention, and he has the math needed to back him up. He is a genius, or, a super nova idea machine.

The more value you bring to the world with your ideas, the more value you will bring to yourself, your family, and your community. This is the first step towards changing the world.

As per me, I am a humble idea-machine who practices daily.

And I love it.

Do tell me how you do. Tell me on Twitter @ClaudiaYoga or at AskClaudiaYoga.com.

And enjoy the ride.

Ready? Let's go.

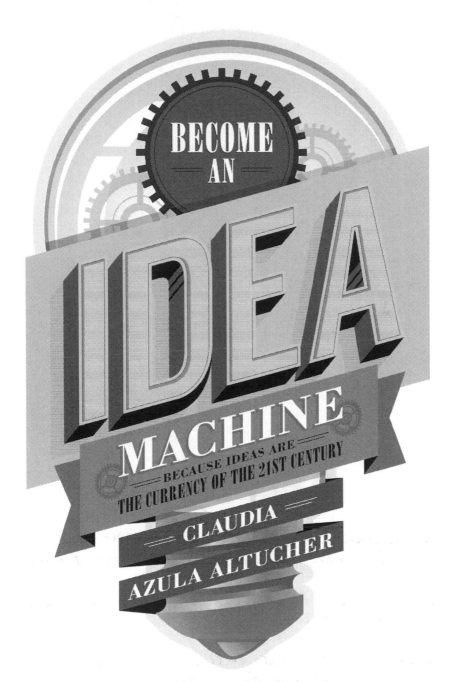

BECOME AN IDEA MACHINE

MACHINE

BECAUSE IDEAS ARE
THE CURRENCY OF THE 21ST CENTURY

CLAUDIA

AZULA ALTUCHER

PART ONE:

THE FIRST 90 DAYS

1) SOLVE 10 HARD
GRATITUDE PROBLEMS

Complaining is draining us as a species. If we leave our minds un-check they become unruly children, screaming for entitlement.

Every complaint however, hides behind a gratitude possibility. That is what solving a hard gratitude problem is all about.

For example: Say that you dislike getting stuck in traffic as you drive every day, think of how you could turn it around into a "thank you". Nobody said it would be easy.

One suggestion is: I am grateful that I live in a city that has so much traffic because that means there is plenty of opportunities here, and I can meet lots of interesting people.

YOUR TURN: *List 10 things that you don't like and then turn them into things you can be grateful for:*

1 I am grateful to disagree with people to keep my mind open to other views and possibilities

2 I am grateful for my pain so I can appreciate the good days

3 I am grateful to eat gluten free so I am more aware of what I fuel my body with

4 I'm grateful for friends who ignore me to show me who's really got my back

5 I'm grateful for those who do things different than me to teach me patience

6 I am grateful for people who make different choices to show me why I stay to my values

7 I'm grateful my parents took me to church weekly to grow my spiritual bond with God

8 I am grateful there's so much I don't know so I can continue to learn and grow

9 I am grateful things change so I don't take joy for granted

10 I am grateful to be around people I can learn from without competition

☐ PHYSICAL   ☐ SPIRITUAL   ☐ EMOTIONAL

I am grateful for uncertainty to keep open to new possibilites and opportunites

I am grateful for no thanks for doing my best to remind myself its just the right way to live my truth.

2) List 10 Apps That
You'd Like To Use

~

I would like to have an app that tracks my period. Well, I'm a woman. I am pretty sure that application is probably already out there, but I don't know that, so it counts.

As long as it helps me, then it is good. Another app I would like is one that would aggregate all services for whenever I land in a new city, so in one stop I could find where to rent a house, get a car, rent a bike, do online shopping and get a ride from the airport.

> **Now your turn:** *List 10 apps you would like to use. It does not matter weather they already exist or not, think of what would be helpful for you in particular.*

1 a journaling prompt app

2 events going on in town

3 National Park app

4 travel journal

5 budgetting

6 price comparison app

7 self guided tours in new cities

8 portfolio critque / feedback

9 art discussions

10 support groups (emotional /situation)

☐ PHYSICAL   ☐ SPIRITUAL   ☐ EMOTIONAL

3) There is always time. Find 10 moments during your day when you could close your eyes and sit quietly (maybe be grateful)

L ately I've been working non-stop and I find it hard to unplug and take a moment for myself. So this is a particularly useful list, one that opens my eyes.

I can, for example, get away from the computer, close the door, and sit in silence for 3 minutes right now. I could do it. But I am not always at my desk with uninterrupted time to write. So it is useful to find other times. The train ride to NYC is long and with sound cancellation headsets I find I can do it, so that is another moment found for my list.

Now your turn: *List 10 moments during an average every-day for you in which you could sit, close your eyes, and maybe exercise the gratitude muscle:*

1 first thing when my alarm sounds

2 in the car before going into work

3 after eating my lunch before going back to work

4 when I get home from work

5 after breakfast

6 before driving to work

7 getting ready for bed

8 right after dinner

9 while I let the dog out

10 during commercials of a show

☐ **PHYSICAL**   ☐ **SPIRITUAL**   ☐ **EMOTIONAL**

4) 10 Coursera courses you would like to take, and what would they have in their curriculum

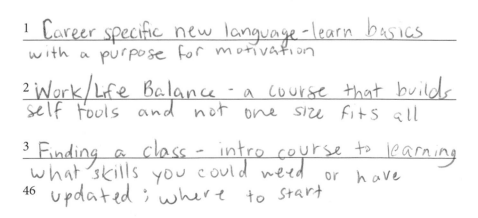

I'm fascinated by our ability to go online and take classes. Coursera is a website that does exactly that, and one course I would like to see is a Yoga class, but done with care, done well.

In their curriculum they would have the ancient scriptures and what they mean for us today, the 8 limbs, the obstacles to yoga, the most important asanas, the pranayama or breathing practice, the five bodies that yoga has identified and how do we get to go inwards, what is kundalini and why should we care? What are the most important things for living a yogi life and so on.

A course like that could have 50 episodes or more! I would love to see it. Hm…. I'm feeling the pull towards execution… Must finish this book first… One thing at the time!

Now, your turn to sweat the idea muscle:
*What are 10 courses you would love to see and take in Coursera
and what is in their curriculum*

1 Career specific new language - learn basics with a purpose for motivation

2 Work/Life Balance - a course that builds self tools and not one size fits all

3 Finding a class - intro course to learning what skills you could need or have updated; where to start

4 Culture awareness - learn new habits or customs from other cultures (as small as state to state)

5 Opposite debate - learn the opposing side of your personal view to understand a fuller picture

6 Sign Language

7 What's Next - a class that helps give you guides to manage steps in life (not road map)

8 Design Industry focused

9 Color Theory and how it changes value

10 Adult Health and wellness with fibro. - What's enough / too much

❑ PHYSICAL   ❑ SPIRITUAL   ❑ EMOTIONAL

5) 10 NEW TECHNOLOGIES
FOR SMART REFRIGERATORS

⌒

My refrigerator keeps breaking down, not cooling, lights going off, ice not working, and it definitely never re-fills itself. What if it could?

One idea I have is to make it be intelligent (by way of an internal computer) and catalogue the foods I usually eat, as well as how long do I keep them in there until I throw them out. So then it could just order them and keep it stocked. How would it order them, it would be from another app I am about to invent. It would also deliver items to my kitchen and place them in the fridge. For zero cost.

Hey, nobody said the ideas have to be all great. They are ideas.

NOW IT'S YOUR TURN:

1 help your meal prep by making a grocery store list

2 give meal suggestions based on content

3 knowing food allergies and restrictions

4 search coupons for commonly bought food

5 help pick food based on budget

6 tips on best storage of food for freshness and lasting

7 calorie tracking

8 locks to keep treats safe or avoid late eating

9 organize fridge by meal ingridients

10 track food eaten during the week to avoid over buying

☐ PHYSICAL   ☐ SPIRITUAL   ☐ EMOTIONAL

6) 10 Ways You Could Make Your Traveling
Easier Next Time You Fly

I am on the road quite a bit and find that I usually pack things I end up not using. This annoys me because I end up carrying a lot of unnecessary weight.

So one thing I could do to improve my travel is keep a bag where I have all "extra" washing and make-up supplies so I don't even have to think of it. And I keep it neatly and reduced to bare necessities.

Another thing I could do is make sure all the bags I use have wheels that move in all four directions because it makes things easier.

Now its your turn:

1 read books on my ipad

2 extra memory cards and no laptop

3 if I'm not doing 2+ rolls - no film camera

4 if a clothing item doesn't go with 2 outfits, doesn't come

5 reduce shoes

6 if I don't use it daily at home I don't need it

7 even when checking a bag, pack like a carry on

8 all bags have wheels

9 under 5hr flight = no pillow (use hoodie)

10 bring empty water bottle

☐ PHYSICAL   ☐ SPIRITUAL   ☐ EMOTIONAL

7) TELL ME YOUR FAVORITE 10 BOOKS OF ALL TIME
AND ONE THING YOU LEARNED FROM EACH

There are books that touch me deeply. For example: *Women Who Run With The Wolves* by Clarissa Pinkola Estés inspires me because it has that "I never saw that before" effect. Every time I re-read it I find something new in it that had escaped me in previous reads. Has that ever happened to you?

One thing I learned from that book is that It's OK to break into Spanish. Me gusta cambiar el lenguaje de vez en cuando. I enjoy changing languages once in a while. I miss Spanish. Es una lengua hermosa.

Another book I like is Eckhart Tolle's *The Power Of Now*. Because it reminds me that this moment is all there is, it helps me to relax the face, release tension from the neck, breathe deeply and plunge into this moment, just as it is.

NOW IS YOUR TURN:

1 She Said Yes - be true to youself

2 Girl, Wash Your Face - keep going

3 Hold Still - people will not always understand you, do it anyways

4 Still Alice - appreciation and patience

5 Milk & Honey - you're never too broken

6 The Geography of Bliss - be happy where you are

7 Lean In - be heard

8 Scrappy Little Nobody - Push past what others say

9 Pancakes in Paris - you control your dreams and goals

10 Small Great Things - do the right thing even if its different or some one else's "wrong"

☐ PHYSICAL   ☐ SPIRITUAL   ☐ EMOTIONAL

8) 10 Movies that Caused a Deep
Impression on You, and Why

Spielberg's E.T. was the first movie that caused a big stir within me, so much so, that I started planning my move to the United States at the age of 13.

But it was not the special effects that got me. No, it was the food.

In the movie I saw that children who did not have a lot of money, as was my case, could still order pizza over a phone and pay with a credit card.

Pizza was a luxury for me growing up, something we did on Sundays, sometimes. My family had to wait 10 years (since I was born) for a phone to be installed in my house. And I did not understand how a piece of plastic could buy anyone food… I had to come here. And I did, at 26.

Now is your turn:

1 Remember The Titans - race and coming together

2 Lion King - childhood memories with my parents

3 Goonies - Friends and adventure

4 Little Rascals - just being a kid

5 The Blindside - doing what you can for someone else

6 Stuck in Love - life's complicated

7 Freedom Writers - creating your own future

8 More Than a Game - teamwork and hardwork

9 Thank You for Smoking - learning to think for yourself with modern meassging

10 The Circle - the glory and danger of technology

☐ PHYSICAL   ☐ SPIRITUAL   ☐ EMOTIONAL

9) 10 WAYS TO IMPROVE TRAVELING IN COACH THAT AN AIRLINE LIKE JETBLUE COULD IMPLEMENT TODAY TO MAKE PEOPLE HAPPIER

I love Jet Blue. I like how they try hard to offer "extra room" in the airplane for 50 bucks more, or how they are incorporating their "mint" service for coast-to-coast flights and they are a lot less, one third, than what the other airlines would charge for a flat bed.

One idea I have is to partner with a cookie company and offer everyone on board a warm chocolate chip or raisin cookie before departure.

WHAT ARE YOUR SUGGESTIONS *so the passengers would feel the love?*

1 offer 30 min of free wifi

2 one complimenery refill on drink

3 in flight movie

4 power outlets

5 if flight delayed - transportation to next gate or luggage

6 give headphones

7 mint or gum

8 give newspapers or puzzles

9 loaded tablet for kids

10 coupon book for destination

❏ **PHYSICAL**   ❏ **SPIRITUAL**   ❏ **EMOTIONAL**

10) 10 Meetups you could
RUN IN YOUR AREA

⟣⟶

Meetups can be great or they can be horrible. I've attended a few where the organizer was so good that everyone got a chance to speak, and he was always introducing people and making sure all of us had a good time. It was a meetup for Argentine people living in New York City and I still have very fond memories of eating ñoquis on the 29th of the month which is an Argentinean tradition where you put money under the plate and then go to town on the ñoquis with red marinara sauce and parmesan. Argentineas have it good faith that this will bring you money for the following month.

Recently people have started organizing *Choose Yourself* meetups. This is happening so much that James has come up with a suggested outline for meetings, which he has on his latest book, *The Choose Yourself Guide To Wealth*, and also on his blog and newsletter.

WHAT ARE YOUR MEET-UP IDEAS *and how can you make sure EVERYONE would participate:*

1 _____

2 _____

3 _____

4 _____

5 _____

6 _____

7 _____

8 _____

9 _____

10 _____

❑ PHYSICAL   ❑ SPIRITUAL   ❑ EMOTIONAL

11) 10 NEW YOGA POSES YOU CAN CREATE, I.E.: USE ANIMAL NAMES, AND DESCRIBE ALIGNMENT, PURPOSE & EFFECTS

O ne time I asked my God-children to come up with a yoga pose on the fly. My godson, who was 7 years-old at the time came up with the "mosquito pose" immediately. He had never heard of inhibitions.

The pose had a noise too. It went like this: 'bzzzzz' and had you standing, half squatting, like a mosquito, flapping your arms. That is the alignment.

The purpose was to have fun, and the effect was that you slowed the breathing down, to keep the buzz sound going.

NOW IS YOUR TURN: *It might help to go 7-year-old on this one:*

1 _____

2 _____

3 _____

4 _____

5 _____

6 _____

7 _____

8 _____

9 _____

10 _____

❏ PHYSICAL   ❏ SPIRITUAL   ❏ EMOTIONAL

12) Locate one character in history you admire (could be Joan of Arc, or Buddha or Eleanor Roosevelt, or Rumi) and write 10 questions you would ask of him or her:

I'd like to meet Buddha. And I have a feeling that once I saw him in person all questions would be wiped out, so I would have to prepare.

One thing I would like to know is how did he manage to keep the politics of the kingdoms around him and the growing number of followers he had from hating each other.

Also, why did he not write down something? Could he not see that his teachings would be a little distorted over time? Did he not care?

Who would you talk to and what are your ten questions? *Pretend you could really talk to them and ask things that really interest you:*

1 _____

2 _____

3 _____

4 _____

5 _____

6 _____

7 _____

8 _____

9 _____

10 _____

❑ PHYSICAL   ❑ SPIRITUAL   ❑ EMOTIONAL

13) List 10 ways you could generate passive income within the next 3 months and the 2nd step that would have to happen for any of them to move ahead

Passive income...

S ounds so good. And the ideas for it seem so hard, but are they? Let's see. I could create an affiliate program with amazon and then create a blog to review products and link, as well as tweet, things that I have used and liked.

It does not say how much I have to make, it just says generate passive income, right?

So the next step would be to create an Amazon affiliate account (which is super easy) and start reviewing things I already use, and linking and spreading. That is one way!

What are ten other ways?

1 _____

2 _____

3 _____

4 _____

5 _____

6 _____

7 _____

8 _____

9 _____

10 _____

❑ PHYSICAL   ❑ SPIRITUAL   ❑ EMOTIONAL

14) Ten ideas for fascinating investigative articles I would like to write

and for what publication

In a fantasy world I would like to write an article about all the ways in which Homeland (the TV show) gets it right and the ways in which it gets it wrong. Meaning, how the CIA really works as opposed to what is fiction.

I would publish it on Brain Pickings. It would be a long piece, six thousand words, thoroughly researched. I would have to get access to the CIA. Hm, that's going to be tough. Good thing this is just ideas.

Actually, they don't even have to be "investigative". They can be any articles, whatever works. Whatever you think you would like to read.

What are your ten, *and where would you publish them?*

1 _____

2 _____

3 _____

4 _____

5 _____

6 _____

7 _____

8 _____

9 _____

10 _____

☐ PHYSICAL   ☐ SPIRITUAL   ☐ EMOTIONAL

15) Ten things I have at home that I don't need which I could either donate and/or throw away or re-purpose

I just took a walk around the house on the way upstairs. I saw some books that I have not touched in over a year, and a couple of towels that have seen better times… One of them has a burn in it, and a hole, I think it even smells.

So that towel could be thrown out, and the books could go to the local library. And the clothes that I no longer use could be donated to the Vietnam Vets (they pick up from your front door in the North East)

This is a particularly useful exercise for me, because I find that whenever I clear out clutter my mind works better.

Clutter free house = clutter free mind

So what are your ten things, *and how could you "recycle" them?*

1 _____

2 _____

3 _____

4 _____

5 _____

6 _____

7 _____

8 _____

9 _____

10 _____

❏ PHYSICAL   ❏ SPIRITUAL   ❏ EMOTIONAL

16) Ten risky things you could do this week
TO GET OUT OF YOUR COMFORT ZONE

A s I mentioned, a few weeks ago I listened to James's podcast with Noah Kagan and I was shocked by how much I live within the safe confines of my soft and cozy comfort zone.

Noah gave a couple of suggestions of small things we could do to up the game and get out of the lethargic state.

One of them was that on the next airplane ride, I would sit on a seat that wasn't assigned to me, and then when the person who was meant to sit there came along, I would just say I'm sorry and move. It seemed like nothing but I was scared to dead when I actually did it on a flight to Florida.

Nothing major happened, but I got out of the comfort zone, my heart beat fast, and I felt alive. Also, I survived. Doing these small challenges gets you "executing". And you only need to write 10 suggestions. Extra bonus if you try one.

Your turn, go:

1 _____

2 _____

3 _____

4 _____

5 _____

6 _____

7 _____

8 _____

9 _____

10 _____

❑ Physical   ❑ Spiritual   ❑ Emotional

17) Ten Ways I can Improve
My Daily "Physical" Practice

I love this one, because it brings me back to the core of what is important in life. Every day we have been focusing on the mental side of the practice and just ticking a box on the bottom of each page for the other three parts, but today we are focusing on the physical part.

Off the top of my head I know I can improve physically, for example, by re-reading a book on yoga anatomy that is excellent (*Functional Yoga Anatomy*, by David Keil). This book helps me because it gives me alignment tips for when I am on the mat.

Another way I could improve is by taking stairs in the subway instead of passively getting on the escalera mecanica. "Moving escalators"? Or by walking instead of driving whenever possible.

What are ten easy, simple ways *in which you can improve the physical part of the daily practice?*

1 _____

2 _____

3 _____

4 _____

5 _____

6 _____

7 _____

8 _____

9 _____

10 _____

❑ PHYSICAL   ❑ SPIRITUAL   ❑ EMOTIONAL

18) Ten Ways I can Improve My Daily "Emotional" Practice The emotional leg of the daily practice has to do with the people I surround myself with.

~

I could for example, as my first idea, think of something I want in my life, and then come up with ways in which I can make that, what I want, happen for another person rather than me.

Another way is that I could call a family member whom I love and with whom I have lost touch, say hello, and see if there is anything I can do for them.

What are your ten?

1 _____

2 _____

3 _____

4 _____

5 _____

6 _____

7 _____

8 _____

9 _____

10 _____

❏ PHYSICAL   ❏ SPIRITUAL   ❏ EMOTIONAL

19) Ten Ways I can Improve
My Daily "Mental" Practice

~~~

Aren't we going through this book already?! Yes we are... And one way to help the mental leg of the practice is to notice complaining.

For example, did it bother you that the past three days we've been having a somewhat repetitive exercise, and that it is focusing on the four legs making tomorrow predictable?

Would you call that complaining? Well, noticing complaining and replacing it with gratitude is one way of improving the mental practice.

Another is to come up with 20 ideas instead of 10, to shake things up.

What are your ten?

1 _____

2 _____

3 _____

4 _____

5 _____

6 _____

7 _____

8 _____

9 _____

10 _____

❏ PHYSICAL   ❏ SPIRITUAL   ❏ EMOTIONAL

20) Ten Ways I can Improve
My Daily "Spiritual" Practice

M y daily contemplation practice starts with sitting in silence, quieting things and then "going beyond thank you".

It is easy to be grateful for the roof over my head, or the love of my husband. I am very grateful for that, but it comes off the top of my head first, it rolls off my tongue, it's a go-to type of gratitude.

When I go past the simple thank you I notice I have new glasses, and I can see clearly. Or, I am not hungry, which is a nice thing.

In going past thank you, *what are ten things you can be grateful for right now?*

1 _____

2 _____

3 _____

4 _____

5 _____

6 _____

7 _____

8 _____

9 _____

10 _____

❑ PHYSICAL   ❑ SPIRITUAL   ❑ EMOTIONAL

21) You are about to be transported into another planet and must write a book to leave your wisdom behind. Come up with 10 ideas of the book titles that you could write, with 3 items that would go in the table of contents.

W e are going away! And all that wisdom gained throughout years of living, where is it going to go?

What have you learned? What can you share? What did you do when all the odds were against you and still, you managed? What are your 10 books?

One I would like to write is: *"The Guide To Asking For Things"* and in the table of contents I would have (a)–How to ask so that you get a yes (b)– how to ask when the odds are against you (c)– how NOT to ask.

What are your ten books *and three things in their contents?*

1 _____

2 _____

3 _____

4 _____

5 _____

6 _____

7 _____

8 _____

9 _____

10 _____

❑ PHYSICAL   ❑ SPIRITUAL   ❑ EMOTIONAL

22) Ten People That Made An
Impact In Your Life and Why

W hen I was 10 my uncle Eduardo took me to see a theater play in Buenos Aires. It was an amazing experience, we had to get dressed, we went to dinner, it was all very special.

The play was Ibsen's "A Dolls House" where I saw, perhaps for the first time, that women could also be strong, maybe even very strong.

My uncle makes it into the top 10 for me, because he showed me another way, early on, and without much fuzz.

He let me reach my own conclusions, never lectured me, and took me out on the town. I had fun.

Who are your ten?

1 _____

2 _____

3 _____

4 _____

5 _____

6 _____

7 _____

8 _____

9 _____

10 _____

☐ PHYSICAL   ☐ SPIRITUAL   ☐ EMOTIONAL

23) 10 LINES YOU HEARD RECENTLY THAT LEFT

YOU WONDERING...AND WHY

Recently I read Tony Robbins book *Money*, and in it, I learned of a time when Robbins was taking martial arts classes from a master, and one night, after repeating a move for 300 times, an exhausted Tony said: Master, when are we moving onto the next move?

The master replied: "Oh grasshopper, this is the next move. The fact that you cannot tell that the way you did it this time and the way you did it before is different tells me you are still a dabbler".

I loved that. It made me realize that this sentence IS my next move. It brought me back to the present with one strike!

WHAT ARE TEN LINES *you heard recently that left you in awe?*

1 _____

2 _____

3 _____

4 _____

5 _____

6 _____

7 _____

8 _____

9 _____

10 _____

❏ PHYSICAL   ❏ SPIRITUAL   ❏ EMOTIONAL

24) COME UP WITH
10 NEW RECIPES.

I love sweet things. And I also love salty things. And I want to eat healthy. Is it asking for much? Recently I realized that I could soak almonds, then chop them and add agave and a lot of good quality salt... Then dehydrate them (or bake them at a low temperature).

They make for wonderful snacks, and may not be the healthiest thing but I like them.

What are some of the flavors you love? Do you like bananas? Are you a chocolate kind of person? Or are you into gourmet meals?

COME UP WITH TEN ORIGINAL RECIPES, *they cannot be the old ones, they have to have something new... your creation. Go:*

1 _____

2 _____

3 _____

4 _____

5 _____

6 _____

7 _____

8 _____

9 _____

10 _____

❏ PHYSICAL   ❏ SPIRITUAL   ❏ EMOTIONAL

25) TEN THINGS I DENY MYSELF

PERMISSION TO BUY, AND WHY

I have some guilty pleasures. I would like for example, to get myself a full day of massage, manicure pedicure, facial and make up. The whole thing.

I've never done it. I think it's because I don't think I can afford the time it would take with so many ideas and projects. Maybe I could if I really wanted to. I don't know.

WHAT IS IN YOUR TEN?

1 _____

2 _____

3 _____

4 _____

5 _____

6 _____

7 _____

8 _____

9 _____

10 _____

☐ PHYSICAL   ☐ SPIRITUAL   ☐ EMOTIONAL

26) Idea Sex: Go back and find the books that made a difference in your life (#7) and then match it with the 10 lines you heard recently and that had an impact on you (#23). Now, come up with a good title based on what you heard and a subtitle based on the books you loved.

~~

This one requires good old thinking and mixing and matching. The line for me was "This IS the next move" and the book can be either *The Power of Now* or *Women Who Run With the Wolves*.

So here is my go at a title and subtitle:

TITLE: *This IS Your Life.*

SUBTITLE: *Because it is happening now*

How is that for title and subtitle?

Idea sex! Go ahead, list your ten:

1 _____

2 _____

3 _____

4 _____

5 _____

6 _____

7 _____

8 _____

9 _____

10 _____

❑ PHYSICAL   ❑ SPIRITUAL   ❑ EMOTIONAL

27) LIST 10 QUORA QUESTIONS THAT YOU FEEL PULLED TO ANSWER, AND WHY.

Quora can be a rabbit hole of sorts, there are a lot of good questions, and some pull me in, I get this feeling that I HAVE to answer... Maybe because I think I know the answer or because I want to make a point, I don't know, I just feel a pull.

If you've never been there you are in for a treat. People from all over the world ask questions away all day long.

Browsing you will see that some of them will grab your attention. List the top 10 and write why they are pulling you in, what would you say...

By the way, you don't have to answer them in Quora, just doing the list here is fine as your idea muscle will be sweating, but if you feel inclined to give Quorans a piece of your wisdom... I am not judging.

WHAT DID YOU FIND?

1 _____

2 _____

3 _____

4 _____

5 _____

6 _____

7 _____

8 _____

9 _____

10 _____

❑ **PHYSICAL**   ❑ **SPIRITUAL**   ❑ **EMOTIONAL**

28) 10 Great titles for "Indie" type of movies and plot

I like independent cinema, for example I recently saw *Begin Again* with Mark Ruffalo and Keira Knightly, about a chance encounter, through music, that leads to the production of an album recorded live on the streets on NYC sprinkled with love and lots of emotional stuff.

Loved that movie. But sometimes Indie movies can get really weird, at least for my taste, for example: *The Royal Tenembaums*, which was, I would say interesting and funny, but a bit strange. We all have different tastes in movies.

The cool part, however, is that we can let the imagination roam free…

One idea I have is to make a movie about a woman who stumbles upon a teleportation machine that allows her to live in a different city of the world every day, but she never knows what city she will wake up on.

What she does realize, however, is that the characters that appear in every city, look different but have the same personalities. And the story repeats until she has a realization. *Groundhog Day* style.

WHAT ARE YOUR TEN TITLES AND PLOTS?

1 _____

2 _____

3 _____

4 _____

5 _____

6 _____

7 _____

8 _____

9 _____

10 _____

☐ PHYSICAL   ☐ SPIRITUAL   ☐ EMOTIONAL

29) Pretend you are an expert and argue 5 reasons why aromatherapy is real and it works, and 5 reasons why it is a scam.

The beauty of the 'for or against' argument is that it expands the mind into looking at places where we normally do not want to look.

I used to be really into all the alternative things I saw around me, and then I guess one day I grew up and noticed that not everything is real. And that I was making myself believe things… Reasoning like this has been very helpful

For example: I can argue that the smell of lavender is nice in my laundry and makes me feel fresh, and I can argue that is just perfume…

Can you argue for or against? *Go ahead, then.*

1 _____

2 _____

3 _____

4 _____

5 _____

6 _____

7 _____

8 _____

9 _____

10 _____

☐ PHYSICAL   ☐ SPIRITUAL   ☐ EMOTIONAL

30) TEN WAYS IN WHICH YOU CAN
IMPROVE YOUR SLEEP.

I don't work well if I don't get my good 9 to 10 hours of sleep. I know, for some this is ridiculous, others – not many - agree. James tells me that the average violinist sleeps for 8.5 hours, I seem to need 9.

Since, regardless of for how long, in the end we all have to sleep or else we die… It might be good to consider how to improve the quality of the sleep we get be it 6, 7 or whatever amount of hours.

I recently learned that having the room be in complete darkness helps a lot, so I got some curtains from Amazon that produce a blackout effect. Then I heard about the blue light of the computer and how bad it is for you after dark, because it inhibits the melatonin production in our brains which is key for sleep. On that, I downloaded an app from f.lux as a suggestion from Dave Asprey (he wrote *The Bulletproof Diet*), and it works. Now the computer knows when the sun has set and the screen turns orange. So far I have not increased the amount of hours I sleep (good thing!) But I find the quality is better.

WHAT ARE TEN WAYS *you could improve your sleep quality?*

1 _____

2 _____

3 _____

4 _____

5 _____

6 _____

7 _____

8 _____

9 _____

10 _____

❏ Physical   ❏ Spiritual   ❏ Emotional

31) TEN TIMES WHEN YOU
LAUGHED OUT LOUD

James makes me laugh every day. But one day in particular he was reading this book *"Food A Love Story"* by Jim Gaffigan and he started laughing out loud non-stop.

I had never seen him like that, and I couldn't help it, I started laughing too, and Josie and Mollie had no choice but to follow, and suddenly the four of us were laughing. And we had no idea why, only James knew.

Later on I read the book, and the chapter where Jim gives instructions on how to "cook" a hot-dog had me in tears because his instructions change depending on weather his wife is around and watching or not. I am still cracking up.

Children laugh 300 times a day. Adults, only 5. What happened?

WHAT ARE TEN MOMENTS *when you remember laughing out loud?*

1 _____

2 _____

3 _____

4 _____

5 _____

6 _____

7 _____

8 _____

9 _____

10 _____

❏ Physical   ❏ Spiritual   ❏ Emotional

32) Ten Uniforms You could wear for
One Day Just to Observe Reactions

~~~

The other day we left a restaurant after brunch and it was suddenly very cold so I borrowed James's doctor's lab coat. We were walking down Main Street and as soon as I put it on I noticed that I felt different. Maybe it was the way people were looking at me, or maybe it was just delusion, I don't know... But something was different.

Now of course, wearing a doctor's lab coat is his idea, not mine... But I wonder if I was to wear a UPS delivery uniform, or I don't know, another visible, recognizable uniform...

What are ten that you could do a dare to see what reactions you get?

Bonus points if you do it. *Tell me about it*
@ClaudiaYoga #IdeaMachineUniform

1 _____

2 _____

3 _____

4 _____

5 _____

6 _____

7 _____

8 _____

9 _____

10 _____

❑ PHYSICAL   ❑ SPIRITUAL   ❑ EMOTIONAL

33) Ten ideas for businesses that children could set outside on a summer afternoon, other than lemonade stands

~

How about if instead of the usual lemonade stand, a child had a sign that said, "I will create your Twitter account" for $2? Or Your Wikipedia page for 10? Or something along those lines?

Don't they come knowing how to operate computers now? As far as I can tell the children around me understand computers much better than I do.

I wonder if they can even imagine what a world without the web would look like... I am pretty sure they can't.

What are 10 ideas *you could offer the kids of today?*

1 _____

2 _____

3 _____

4 _____

5 _____

6 _____

7 _____

8 _____

9 _____

10 _____

☐ **PHYSICAL**   ☐ **SPIRITUAL**   ☐ **EMOTIONAL**

34) THINK OF TEN COMPANIES YOU USE OFTEN. AND THEN FIND THE ONES THAT ACTUALLY TRADE ON THE STOCK EXCHANGE. AND WHY DO YOU USE THEM?

F or example, I use Amazon every day, all the time, and Google, and both are on the stock market. I use them because Amazon is to me like the global supermarket, and Google is just Google…

WHAT ARE COMPANIES, *other than the obvious ones I just listed,*
that you use all the time that are listed on an exchange?

1 _____

2 _____

3 _____

4 _____

5 _____

6 _____

7 _____

8 _____

9 _____

10 _____

❏ Physical   ❏ Spiritual   ❏ Emotional

35) TEN CITIES YOU WOULD LIKE TO VISIT AND ONE THING

YOU WOULD LIKE TO SEE IN EACH OF THEM.

I've never been to Kyoto in Japan, or Japan at all for that matter, and I understand they have great temples.

Another place I would like to visit: Varanasi, on the banks of the river Ganga in India. People say you can feel the "spirit" in it. Or at least that is how I understand it.

WHAT ARE TEN PLACES YOU WOULD LIKE TO GO TO
(other than the ones I mentioned) and why?

1 _____

2 _____

3 _____

4 _____

5 _____

6 _____

7 _____

8 _____

9 _____

10 _____

❑ PHYSICAL   ❑ SPIRITUAL   ❑ EMOTIONAL

36) Funny Answers: Come up with 10 ideas for questions at the level of 3rd grade tests, and then funny answers

I confess, I saw this one in a book. It had the famous algebra problem that goes "solve for "x"" and someone had circled the "x" in the question and then wrote: There it is…

WHAT ARE TEN FUNNY ANSWERS *to test questions you've heard before or that you can come up with?*

1 _____

2 _____

3 _____

4 _____

5 _____

6 _____

7 _____

8 _____

9 _____

10 _____

❏ PHYSICAL ❏ SPIRITUAL ❏ EMOTIONAL

37) Ten Reasons Why You Think Adults Only Laugh
5 Times A Day (Instead of 300)

W hy I wonder is it that as adults we don't laugh as much as our little counterparts? I could say that the responsibilities of daily life weigh on us. True, then again, just thinking of coming up with things that make me laugh in a prior list, MADE me laugh.

Is it really that difficult?

What are ten reasons *that stopped the laughter for you?*

1 _____

2 _____

3 _____

4 _____

5 _____

6 _____

7 _____

8 _____

9 _____

10 _____

❑ PHYSICAL   ❑ SPIRITUAL   ❑ EMOTIONAL

38) Game Time. Create ten simple
card games and tell the rules.

I love the Argentinean game of Truco, because it is all about lying and being loud and intimidating. The game is all about interaction, conversation and out-witting the adversary. So I am going to come up with one inspired on that.

Everyone pulls a card and the one who thinks has the highest number yells LOUD! And if they were wrong they get five points taken away, but if they were right they get 10 points. Whoever stays quiet, if they were wrong they get 3 points subtracted, and if they right they get the only 4 added.

Game goes to 100 points. First to reach the 100 points wins.

What are your ten games?

1 _____

2 _____

3 _____

4 _____

5 _____

6 _____

7 _____

8 _____

9 _____

10 _____

☐ **PHYSICAL**   ☐ **SPIRITUAL**   ☐ **EMOTIONAL**

39) Ten ways in which you could surprise a loved one,

WHICH THEY WOULD LIKE

I like surprising James. I sometimes write him a card that he will see only when he gets to his computer in the morning. I plan it carefully; I need to make sure he has left the computer for the day (not easy!). Then I fill it with hearts or a love note.

Then I wait for the kisses in the morning. My reward.

WHAT ARE TEN WAYS *you could surprise someone in your life, your kids, or partner or co-worker, in a way THEY will like it?*

1 _____

2 _____

3 _____

4 _____

5 _____

6 _____

7 _____

8 _____

9 _____

10 _____

❏ PHYSICAL   ❏ SPIRITUAL   ❏ EMOTIONAL

40) Ten Regrets of the Past you Could Let Go Of.

Sometimes I regret that when I first came to the United States I got a job (because I wanted to feed myself) instead of pursuing my dreams of acting on Broadway. I even got to audition for the Broadway production of *Evita* once...

After the audition one of the people in the panel wanted to speak with me, he asked me if I was from Buenos Aires, but I knew I had been terrible in my singing so I just run away.

Later I realized that I am not a very good actress, because showing my deep emotions in public makes me embarrassed, so I am pretty sure it was for the best.

And that means that I could let go of that regret.

What are ten regrets *you could let go of today? Notice I say you "could". It does not mean you have to, although it might be nice.*

1 _____

2 _____

3 _____

4 _____

5 _____

6 _____

7 _____

8 _____

9 _____

10 _____

❏ PHYSICAL   ❏ SPIRITUAL   ❏ EMOTIONAL

41) Ten Ways You Can Improve
Your Work Situation Today

⌒

We all work differently, some from home, some in a cubicle, some on the road. No matter what there are always ways to improve our rituals around it, or how we eat, or how we make sure we take rest and so on.

For example, I know that if I do my breathing practice in the morning with all the rituals (without skipping anything) I tend to have laser focus later on when I am either writing or making videos or teaching yoga. So that is one idea: to not skip my breathing practice.

Another one I've been looking into is the walking machine for when I am writing so I am not always sitting. This one has me thinking a lot about the pros and cons, I fear I may get tired of it and avoid both walking and writing. So I am still not sure. But hey! It's an idea.

What are ten *that could improve your day "today"?*

1 _____

2 _____

3 _____

4 _____

5 _____

6 _____

7 _____

8 _____

9 _____

10 _____

❑ **PHYSICAL**   ❑ **SPIRITUAL**   ❑ **EMOTIONAL**

42) Suppose a friend was selling her car and you wanted to give her ten tips on how to write copy so that it sells. Write the 10 tips

I'd suggest keeping it short and keeping it real, yet highlighting the good things about the car, i.e.: low mileage.

What are your ten ideas? *If a car does not work for you, you can think of a house, or anything. But do provide ten ideas to sell better:*

1 _____

2 _____

3 _____

4 _____

5 _____

6 _____

7 _____

8 _____

9 _____

10 _____

❏ PHYSICAL   ❏ SPIRITUAL   ❏ EMOTIONAL

43) Ten Business Ideas
That Could Help The Elder.

$\rightsquigarrow$

The population of older people is rising. They need services. For example: They need caretakers and there could be an app that solved that.

Or there should be a business of medical advocates, where if you are in a hospital and the doctors only care that you live, but not much about your quality of life, then your advocates would liaise between family and the medical establishment, making everyone feel at ease.

What are ten ideas you have?

1 _____

2 _____

3 _____

4 _____

5 _____

6 _____

7
_____

8
_____

9
_____

10
_____

❏ PHYSICAL   ❏ SPIRITUAL   ❏ EMOTIONAL

44) TEN IDEAS ON HOW YOU CAN
GET MORE OUT OF YOUR DOLLAR

I like using money efficiently. And there is no better practice for this than a good old hussle and bargain.

When in India I fought the rickshaw drivers for 15 cents, and discussed the price of towels in shop to bring it down another 10 cents. It was not about the money, clearly, it was about the fact that in that culture that is how they do things. If you are not bargaining then they think they can take advantage of you, especially in a small community around a yoga studio where you are clearly the foreigner.

Since then I ask for discounts all the time, especially when I buy a dress I like, and most of the time I get them.

WHAT ARE TEN IDEAS *you could use today to get more value out of each of your hard earned dollars?*

1 _____

2 _____

3 _____

4 _____

5 _____

6 _____

7 _____

8 _____

9 _____

10 _____

❏ PHYSICAL   ❏ SPIRITUAL   ❏ EMOTIONAL

45) Ten memories you could create with your loved ones for the next holiday
INSTEAD OF FOLLOWING THE HERD.

I'm a Grinch. I hate Christmas because I cannot stand the constant psycho playing of carols everywhere, like in Grand Central, and also, the shopping induced panic that takes over our culture.

So I've created a gratitude ritual around our family whereby, we hold hands, the four of us, and each member can say something they are grateful for.

I can't stop Christmas, and that is OK, but I can create a new memory around it that reflects more of my personal values than on what comes from the outside.

What are ten ideas *of memories you could create*
with your loved ones, around a holiday theme, and make it yours?

1 _____

2 _____

3 _____

4 _____

5 _____

6 _____

7 _____

8 _____

9 _____

10 _____

☐ PHYSICAL   ☐ SPIRITUAL   ☐ EMOTIONAL

46) Your idea muscle is pretty warm by now; It's time for the 100X challenge. List One hundred things you are grateful for today.

～～

Going past "thank you" is a sure way to notice how much we already have in our lives that goes unnoticed.

Listing just ten things that we are grateful for is easy. For me it just rolls out of my tongue: James, the girls, my god children, my friends, health, love, my family, a roof over my head, food, doing work I love, relative intelligence, ideas, my tribe, newsletter subscribers, yoga, peace, and on and on. Easy.

One hundred however, by definition will make you go past the "easy thank you" and notice things like "hot water" or the amazing technology that is probably in your hands or nearby in your phone (I am grateful for the metronome app that helps with breathing counts!). One hundred: Go! You have half a page here, fill the whole thing if you have to; margins are a go, and just do it, don't worry about lines, think outside of the margins.

47) Ten things you would do if you were 17 again, and you had 20K to spend for a year.

How would you explore?
What could you do?

⟶

I always wanted to leave Buenos Aires. I wanted to see the world, and I wanted it badly. So if I was 17 and had that kind of money I would definitely buy a ticket to anywhere.

The challenge here is to be specific and plan ten things to do for a year with that money and the energy of that youth. So I would go to India, for yoga, for a year, spend little money and go on a road trip, exploring temples and such. I'd also study with different teachers, and just have fun. That is one idea.

What are your ten?

1 _____

2 _____

3 _____

4 _____

5 _____

6 _____

7 _____

8 _____

9 _____

10 _____

☐ PHYSICAL ☐ SPIRITUAL ☐ EMOTIONAL

48) List ten people you would like to have as mentors today. Then write one question you would like to ask them.

⌒

I am pretty fond of people who are very smart. I would choose Peter Thiel today because his book made me look at the world differently (competition for example, and how he sees it as totally counter-productive, was an aha! moment for me).

In his book *Zero To One* he poses a difficult question. He says: what is one thing you know to be true that people would not want to accept? And that is what I would ask him, today. What is the one thing he discovered recently which he knows to be true and that he thinks people would not accept right away? Or if that is too obvious I can think of another question I like: "What took you the longest to understand"?

There are so many people I'd love to have as mentors: Cheryl Richardson, Tony Robbins, the list goes on.

What are your ten proposed mentors *and what is the one question you would ask? Today.*

1 _____

2 _____

3 _____

4 _____

5 _____

6 _____

7 _____

8 _____

9 _____

10 _____

❏ PHYSICAL   ❏ SPIRITUAL   ❏ EMOTIONAL

49) WHAT ARE TEN THINGS THAT TOOK YOU THE LONGEST TO UNDERSTAND?

I had a lot of trouble understanding that I could not "buy" my worth. For example: I made a really stupid mistake once, when I thought that I would get a marriage proposal if I bought a home.

Thing is I saw it on TV. It was in the HBO show "Sex And The City" where Miranda, the independent lawyer, got a marriage proposal the minute she closed on her home. She called it Murphy's Law. I call it *delusion*, but that is now, not then… Because back then I rushed and bought myself a home in the suburbs in an unconscious attempt to repeat her fortune.

Of course my marriage proposal came exactly three months after I SOLD that house, and after five years of sweating the repairs of a home I could not afford. Lesson learned. Expensive as hell.

WHAT ARE TEN THINGS *that took you a long time to understand?*

1 _____

2 _____

3 _____

4 _____

5 _____

6 _____

7 _____

8 _____

9 _____

10 _____

☐ PHYSICAL   ☐ SPIRITUAL   ☐ EMOTIONAL

50) TEN THINGS THAT
MAKE TALENT HAPPEN.

~~~

Is talent a gift? I don't think so. Talent might be part of it but it is not all. When Michael Jordan was deemed too short for basketball in his sophomore year he decided to take 1000 basketball shots a day. By the time his height caught up with him he was more than ready. He has said: *I can accept failure, everyone fails at something. But I can't accept not trying.*

So that is one thing that helps talent, repetition, trying, and preparation.

WHAT ARE TEN OTHER THINGS? *Think hard on this one; don't give me ten versions of repetition or practice, but rather look deeply into what other things can factor in on it?*

1 _____

2 _____

3 _____

4 _____

5 _____

6 _____

7 _____

8 _____

9 _____

10 _____

❑ PHYSICAL   ❑ SPIRITUAL   ❑ EMOTIONAL

51) IDEA SEX: REMEMBER THE TEN PEOPLE YOU'D LIKE TO HAVE AS MENTORS?

Choose one and come up with ten ideas of things to do so that when you finally ask them for coffee, or meet them at an event, they will say "yes"

What does it take to get someone you don't know to talk to you? Because, let's be clear, it is *not* just asking. In fact, asking in cold, without any preparation can, and will hurt you. The person might label you as "annoying" or "out of touch".

Asking cold never works. Networking needs years of preparation. And we can help it a lot by for example, by reading everything they write. And then listening, and trying their ideas… So then, when we email this person, or when we meet them at an event, we are prepared, and we have something to say that will peak THEIR interest. For example I admire many yoga teachers and wanted to ask some to come on my yoga podcast. Many have said yes and it is mostly because they know I have read all of their books and reviewed them in Amazon.

WHAT ARE TEN WAYS *in which you can prepare to meet the mentor of your dreams?*

1 _____

2 _____

3 _____

4 _____

5 _____

6 _____

7 _____

8 _____

9 _____

10 _____

❑ PHYSICAL   ❑ SPIRITUAL   ❑ EMOTIONAL

52) Ten reasons why a young person needs to see Las Vegas and ten reasons

WHY IT MIGHT BE BEST TO STAY AWAY.

It's Vegas. It's fun, and it's evil, and it's the land of opportunity or the land of distraction and deception, and the shows are amazing, but then again…

If you are advising someone very young,

what are your ten reasons pro and against visiting such a town?

1 _____

2 _____

3 _____

4 _____

5 _____

6 _____

7 _____

8 _____

9 _____

10 _____

AGAINST

1 _____

2 _____

3 _____

4 _____

5 _____

6 _____

7 _____

8 _____

9 _____

10 _____

❏ PHYSICAL   ❏ SPIRITUAL   ❏ EMOTIONAL

53) Ten Phrases In Which You Lay Down Your Wisdom For Generations to Come

"Be the change" said Gandhi… And we all get it. "Kindness is my religion" said the Dali Lama. "What others think of me is non of my business," said Eleanor Roosevelt, you go woman!

What are ten that you can say to pass over for generations down?

I came up with this one: "Goals are not meant to be achieved, they are meant so we can discover the theme of our lives".

Yes, I know, you probably heard James say that. I can't quite share with him my "wisdom-downloads" because he absorbs it all and runs with it. He wrote about it before I even had a chance. Then again, who is writing an "idea machine" book now?

What are your ten? *Lay your wisdom on us. Heck write a post if you feel inclined to; I would love to read these ten:*

1 _____

2 _____

3 _____

4 _____

5 _____

6 _____

7 _____

8 _____

9 _____

10 _____

❑ PHYSICAL   ❑ SPIRITUAL   ❑ EMOTIONAL

54) TEN WAYS IN WHICH IDEAS
ARE THE NEW CURRENCY?

I deas are the new black. Or maybe the new orange. I picture ideas as bright orange; maybe because of the fruits we ate as primates and how we liked the sweet taste. I think of mangos and papayas. Hm…Delicious, and they are all orange.

But how are ideas like currency?

When someone told me the Hawaiian saying "bless that which you want" it turned my whole life around because I stopped the envy, and realized I needed to cultivate good in me. It was just an *idea* but the *effect* it had on me brought me to a better place where I do work I love. And that is worth even more than money to me.

WHAT ARE TEN WAYS *in which you can see good ideas flourishing as abundance and wealth in your life?*

1 _____

2 _____

3 _____

4 _____

5 _____

6 _____

7 _____

8 _____

9 _____

10 _____

❑ PHYSICAL   ❑ SPIRITUAL   ❑ EMOTIONAL

55) Ten crazy ideas

⤳

Sam Pink, the author, wrote to James one day. He is an unusual type of person, as writers tend to be.

He said he had an idea of making a *microwave that works on the outside.* "Think about it", he wrote… His idea still haunts me.

One I have is: what if everyone suddenly took responsibility for their own lives and stopped the blaming and complaining, what would happen? Crazy right?

What are your ten?

1 _____

2 _____

3 _____

4 _____

5 _____

6 _____

7 _____

8 _____

9 _____

10 _____

❑ PHYSICAL   ❑ SPIRITUAL   ❑ EMOTIONAL

56) Invent ten new words in Spanish
and say what they mean

~~

S panish... It sounds so direct, and so harsh sometimes, and also kind of pretty.

I have an unfair advantage here, I realize. So I will come up with a new word in French. For you it's still Spanish.

My word in French is "d'agiter-er" It means un-stress, or get rid of your agitation. If you say it out loud make sure to use the French "r" in the right way.

Now back to Spanish, what are your ten new words, and what do they mean? And if French sounded better to you then go for it. Choose the language yourself. Do the ideas though.

Do share with me please *on Twitter*
@ClaudiaYoga #IdeaMuscleSpanish

1 _____

2 _____

3 _____

4 _____

5 _____

6 _____

7 _____

8 _____

9 _____

10 _____

❏ PHYSICAL   ❏ SPIRITUAL   ❏ EMOTIONAL

57) Ten Ways In Which I Can Get Myself to Write My Ten Ideas on Days I Don't Want to

W e've all been there. As the British say: It happens to the best of us. We all have "those days". Let's prepare for them.

I know one way that works for me is to announce on Twitter that I am about to write my ten ideas. Then there is no way out. I have to because otherwise I feel like a fraud.

Having a buddy, meaning someone that keeps you accountable is a great idea too…

What are other ideas, list your ten:

1 _____

2 _____

3 _____

4 _____

5 _____

6

_____

7

_____

8

_____

9

_____

10

_____

☐ PHYSICAL   ☐ SPIRITUAL   ☐ EMOTIONAL

58) Ten people I could introduce by way of "permission networking" and why WOULD THEY BOTH BENEFIT?

～

Networking only works when it is done by permission. Otherwise it hurts everyone, because nobody wants to receive an email saying: "hey you should meet Sally because I think so"… that is lazy and unproductive.

Networking done right takes work. So we are going to think today about how it could add value to both parties.

I teach at a local yoga studio that is always looking for teachers to give weekend workshops. And I interview teachers on my yoga podcast.

So recently I thought I would send an email PRIVATELY to a yoga teacher I interviewed and ask him if he would be interested (and if his tour would bring him to this area of the country) in teaching here. If he says yes I a make the intro. I also gave him an out. I said, "You don't need to respond if not interested"… He didn't answer. But I interview many teachers. Who knows? Maybe one will say yes and I can make a permission-networking intro.

What are the ten connections *you could make and how would they benefit from meeting each other?*

1 _____

2 _____

3 _____

4 _____

5 _____

6 _____

7 _____

8 _____

9 _____

10 _____

☐ PHYSICAL   ☐ SPIRITUAL   ☐ EMOTIONAL

59) 10 COMMON EXCUSES PEOPLE USE AND HOW COULD THEY BE TRANSFORMED?

You probably hear them all the time 'I don't have the time', or 'I am not flexible'.

I actually like that one, the one where people tell me 'I am not flexible so I can't do yoga' because I have a perfect answer… Flexibility is of the mind, not the body. With practice flexibility comes.

WHAT ARE TEN EXCUSES *you hear all the time and 10 good come backs for them.*

1 _____

2 _____

3 _____

4 _____

5 _____

6 _____

7
_____

8
_____

9
_____

10
_____

❏ PHYSICAL ❏ SPIRITUAL ❏ EMOTIONAL

60) Ten ways in which I can make
MYSELF MORE RESILIENT.

R e·sil·ient /rə'zilyənt/ adjective (of a substance or object) able to recoil or spring back into shape after bending, stretching, or being compressed.

I love Wikipedia.

I know that when I fast one day during the week, on a random day, it tends to make my body more aware of what I am eating. I've been doing this for so long now that it has become a habit. I miss my fasts now, that is how good they are for me. And they are not even that long… I just, for example, eat early on a Sunday night, and then don't eat until noon on Monday, and that is pretty good.

WHAT ARE TEN THINGS *you can do*
to make yourself more resilient?

1 _____

2 _____

3 _____

4 _____

5 _____

6 _____

7 _____

8 _____

9 _____

10 _____

❏ PHYSICAL   ❏ SPIRITUAL   ❏ EMOTIONAL

61) Ten Things You Would Like Cars To Have as "Add On" Features

I like my car, and I like how they keep on coming better every year. Recently James told me that cars are just computers with a car app on top of them, and I thought that was a very interesting way of looking at it. After all, now I can connect my phone to the car and stream podcasts, make phone calls, and even get re-routed with virtual and up to date maps.

However, there are things that could be better. One idea I have is a very practical addition. I would like for the car to have a button that would shake it, as if it was a dog, and get all the snow out of it, whenever we get hit by one of those tremendous northeastern storms.

What are other things *you would like your car to do?*
And remember to go crazy here; let it do what you really want it to do:

1 _____

2 _____

3 _____

4 _____

5 _____

6 _____

7 _____

8 _____

9 _____

10 _____

❑ PHYSICAL   ❑ SPIRITUAL   ❑ EMOTIONAL

62) WRITE TEN ONE-LINE JOKES AND HAVE ONE PERSON LAUGH AT ONE OF THEM

I would love to be a comedian, but it really takes a lot of work. Louis CK recently said it takes 20 years to make a good one, if they make it, and he was very clear on the "if" part.

But coming up with one-liners that make people laugh is not only fun is also useful. Laughter makes people bond easier and these thinking experiments can lead to better icebreakers for meetings.

I thought of one line the other day and I run it by James, and he laughed, so it qualifies. I said: *"Wine is really good for you, because it has rhynoceront in it."*

In all fairness when I repeated the line three months later he did *not* laugh. I've a feeling the first time he laughed because we had been watching videos of Amy Schumer, and she is funny. Go figure… But if you get even one laugh, during the next week, with any of the lines on the list then you get extra points. Also, and this is totally selfish, I would love to hear it, so tweet it to me @ClaudiaYoga #FunnyIdeaMachine.

WHAT ARE YOUR ONE-LINERS?

1 _____

2 _____

3 _____

4 _____

5 _____

6 _____

7 _____

8 _____

9 _____

10 _____

❑ PHYSICAL   ❑ SPIRITUAL   ❑ EMOTIONAL

63) 10 Things You Could Teach
Young People in 6 Seconds

Vine is the app that younger generations communicate through. And it only gives you six seconds to express yourself in video, that's it.

A few years ago I noticed that my stepdaughters had trouble understanding how the oven works and how to bake a frozen pizza safely.

My idea would be to use each half second to have one of the steps required in, checking the writing in the box for the temperature, noticing how long, opening the box, taking it out, putting it into aluminum foil on top of a surface that can go in the oven, setting the temperature, turning the oven on, waiting till it's warm, putting it in, and taking it out safely (no burns!). I would probably close it with a smile, or maybe even taking a bite of the pizza if it's cheat day (cheat day is the day I allow myself to eat a lot of carbs, usually Saturdays).

So, if you had six seconds to teach something to tweens, *or even adults. What would you teach?*

1 _____

2 _____

3 _____

4 _____

5 _____

6 _____

7 _____

8 _____

9 _____

10 _____

◻ Physical ◻ Spiritual ◻ Emotional

64) TEN THINGS YOU WISH YOU KNEW
BEFORE YOU TURNED 25

If you are younger than 25, I am so jealous, subtract 5 years from your current age and go from there.

There are so many things I wish I really understood before 25. Things that could have saved me some grief, like for example, understanding, really getting it, that my worth is not related to money or to possessions or the things I do. To know that I have value in me, especially if I am coming with 10 ideas a day.

I wonder where I would be today if I had started the practice of the 10 ideas back then. Maybe I would be a supernova idea machine. Who knows? It doesn't really matter because regrets are not conducive to growth, so let's focus on these ten ideas for the day.

WHAT ARE THE TEN THINGS *you would tell that younger you?*

1 _____

2 _____

3 _____

4 _____

5 _____

6 _____

7 _____

8 _____

9 _____

10 _____

❑ PHYSICAL   ❑ SPIRITUAL   ❑ EMOTIONAL

65) List Ten People outside of your inner circle, and outside of your immediate comfort zone, that you would like to meet and why?

—

I find this exercise useful because it takes me out of my inner circle but not too far out. So for example, if I said I would like to meet Angelina Jolie that may be next to impossible as there are too many gatekeepers around her, and she is a top celebrity. However, there are other people who may not be so hard to meet.

For example, I recently noticed that one of the most famous and important yoga mantras, the Gayatri, is featured in the music that opens the show Battlestar Galactica. The composer is Richard Gibbs, and I would like to interview him for my podcast. That is the person and the reason.

The criteria for outside of the inner circle would be that you have never met them in person before (or if you did it was from a distance, at an event).

THE REASON WHY IS MORE IMPORTANT, *because it will point towards the themes of things that are interesting to you right now. Who are your ten and why?*

1 _____

2 _____

3 _____

4 _____

5 _____

6 _____

7 _____

8 _____

9 _____

10 _____

❑ PHYSICAL ❑ SPIRITUAL ❑ EMOTIONAL

66) IF YOU HAD ABSOLUTELY NO WORRIES ABOUT MONEY, AND NO FEAR, WHAT ARE TEN THINGS YOU WOULD DO THIS WEEK?

Note that you cannot just create something like "world peace," you can't buy that. What you do have is unlimited resources, but not a magic wand, and world peace cannot, realistically be created by magic.

So if you wanted to create something as big as world peace, then you would need to provide the ten steps you would do next. That way we bring it back to reality.

One thing I would like to do is invite people to sit in silence, and to rest and meditate and do yoga. I would have all expenses paid and organize it in a way that would maximize the possibility of people who choose to participate, to explore what being in silence means and how it might or might not help them.

WHAT ARE YOUR TEN IDEAS?

1 _____

2 _____

3 _____

4 _____

5 _____

6 _____

7 _____

8 _____

9 _____

10 _____

❑ PHYSICAL   ❑ SPIRITUAL   ❑ EMOTIONAL

67) Ten New Drugs pharmaceuticals could create in the next five years. List the names

AND EFFECTS AND SIDE EFFECTS.

I know I'd like the *creativity drug*, one that keeps me inspired. Hey! These are just ideas, so why not? I would call it "creatinax". Side effects could include insomnia, because you would get so fired up by your projects that going to sleep could be difficult.

You can come up with any ideas, they don't need to be FDA approved, or follow any regulations, at this stage they are just ideas.

WHAT ARE YOUR TEN?

1 _____

2 _____

3 _____

4 _____

5 _____

6 _____

7 _____

8 _____

9 _____

10 _____

❑ PHYSICAL   ❑ SPIRITUAL   ❑ EMOTIONAL

68) Ten Ways in which we will be using TECHNOLOGY DIFFERENTLY IN TEN YEARS.

⌇

M aybe the Google car will be ready and we will be able to go anywhere without having to drive?

Maybe the Internet will be free and available everywhere, even a constitutional right?

What are your ten futuristic ideas?

1 _____

2 _____

3 _____

4 _____

5 _____

6 _____

7 _____

8
_____

9
_____

10
_____

☐ Physical   ☐ Spiritual   ☐ Emotional

69) SOMEONE RECENTLY ASKED: WHAT IS THE ANSWER TO EVERYTHING IN THE UNIVERSE IN JUST ONE WORD.

The book: *Hitchhikers Guide to the Galaxy* says the answer is 42. I came up with the word "now" for an answer, because I believe everything happens right now and the rest is just projections or regrets.

COME UP WITH YOUR TOP TEN WORDS

and give one reason why you chose it:

1 _____

2 _____

3 _____

4 _____

5 _____

6 _____

7

8

9

10

❏ PHYSICAL   ❏ SPIRITUAL   ❏ EMOTIONAL

70) Come up with the title of ten books (fiction or non-fiction) that include a color in the title where the color means something else.

꜀꜀꜀

For example: *"50 Shades of Grey"* or a self-help book called: *"Red. Time to Change Career Direction"*. James came up with that one, he put emphasis on the period after red, as if it was an important sign, making red take on a whole new meaning.

Go for it, *you don't have to write the book, just make up titles:*

1 _____

2 _____

3 _____

4 _____

5 _____

6 _____

7 _____

8 _____

9 _____

10 _____

❑ PHYSICAL   ❑ SPIRITUAL   ❑ EMOTIONAL

71) What is in your "I did" list for today.

To *do* lists keep us all stressed out, trying to fit things into a day that is likely already crammed.

The beauty of an "I did" list is that it releases happy chemicals in the brain as we get a sense of accomplishment.

If it is early in the morning you may want to keep this list as a night exercise. It is a great eye-opener when it comes to how much we actually do get done during any given day. If you think you may forget to do the list at night, then you could alternatively do the I did list for yesterday.

One of the things in my I Did list for me is that I wrote ten ideas for lists for this book and it is only 8:00 AM. I am already feeling good. I did lists tend to get bigger than ten, if so, go on, keep going…

If you are especially proud of something you did tweet to me @ClaudiaYoga #IdeaMachineIDid

What is in your: 'I did' list?

1 _____

2 _____

3 _____

4 _____

5 _____

6 _____

7 _____

8 _____

9 _____

10 _____

❑ PHYSICAL   ❑ SPIRITUAL   ❑ EMOTIONAL

72) WRITE TEN THINGS THAT COME TO MIND WHEN YOU HEAR EACH OF THE FOLLOWING TERMS.

This is a slightly different way of exercising the idea muscle because it requires a little surrendering to whatever your mind may "fire" when it is not being filtered.

For example: When I hear "Writing" I hear myself say: inspiration, sometimes, play, work, sitting, back, reading, prize, books, amazon, James, think...

The trick is to not censor your flow of words.

You can ask someone to read the words to you so you can hear them, or read the words and go, then write the first thing that comes into your mind and don't lift the pen and paper, just let them come out.

IF ANYTHING SURPRISES YOU *tweet to me*

@ClaudiaYoga #IdeaMachineSurprise

1) Passive income: (your ten)

2) Adding value:

3) Going the extra mile:

4) Offering something:

5) Teaching something that will help: _____

6) Giving: _____

7) Grateful: _____

8) Want: _____

9) Need: _____

10) Muse: _____

☐ PHYSICAL   ☐ SPIRITUAL   ☐ EMOTIONAL

73) Ten People You Know but have not been in touch lately, whom you could call TODAY AND WHAT IS THE ONE THING YOU COULD SAY TO CHEER THEM UP.

It does not mean you actually have to do it, you just have to list them and say what you would say to them so that they are happy to hear from you.

I could call my uncle and tell him how much I respect him and how grateful I am he took me to a theater play when I was 10.

Who are your ten *and what would you say?*

1 _____

2 _____

3 _____

4 _____

5 _____

6 _____

7 _____

8 _____

9 _____

10 _____

❏ Physical   ❏ Spiritual   ❏ Emotional

74) WHAT ARE TEN AREAS OF LIFE IN WHICH YOU HAVE CHANGED YOUR MIND?

I used to think that people who commit suicide would have to do life all over again. They would have to come back to life, get into the exact same painful situations, all the way to the brink of desperation, and then choose again weather they would live or not. And this would keep on happening until they learned their lesson and stayed alive.

I've changed my mind on this.

Before, I just "liked" thinking this way due to anger because of my own life while growing up and the circumstances that surrounded me.

Now I realize that depression is a very desperate situation, and people who take their own lives cannot really see any other option. So I think people who are depressed need a lot of help.

WHAT ARE TEN AREAS *where you used to think in one way and then you changed your mind?*

1 _____

2 _____

3 _____

4 _____

5 _____

6 _____

7 _____

8 _____

9 _____

10 _____

❏ PHYSICAL   ❏ SPIRITUAL   ❏ EMOTIONAL

75) Pick One Person you admire. Maybe an actor, maybe a writer, maybe a politician, maybe a film director, maybe a teacher. What is she or he about?

Write ten things that reflect what you think he or she is "all about".

I admire Tony Robbins because I think he is all about helping others, about giving people the tools so they can make effective decisions, about breaking down difficult situations into smaller things so they are more manageable, about bringing the target closer so it is more attainable, about finding experts and interviewing them, about integrity, about showmanship, about transformation, about the power of the messages we tell ourselves, about change, about serving many.

What is one person you admire
and ten things they are all about?

1 _____

2 _____

3 _____

4 _____

5 _____

6 _____

7 _____

8 _____

9 _____

10 _____

❏ PHYSICAL   ❏ SPIRITUAL   ❏ EMOTIONAL

76) TEN BEST FICTION BOOKS YOU READ, WITH ONE DETAIL YOU LIKED ABOUT THEM.

M y favorite fiction book was "*Artemito y la Princesa*." I read it when I was 10, and I loved it because it was about a dragon, Artemito, who had no friends of his same age, and that was my case as well, summers were a very isolated time for me.

WHAT ARE YOUR TOP TEN FICTION BOOKS

and why did they touch you?

1 _____

2 _____

3 _____

4 _____

5 _____

6 _____

7 _____

8 _____

9 _____

10 _____

☐ PHYSICAL   ☐ SPIRITUAL   ☐ EMOTIONAL

77) TEN BEST BLOGPOSTS
I'VE READ AND WHY

⌒

There are blogposts and then there are blogposts. That is the time we live in. I remember reading James's "how to be the luckiest person alive" and how it resonated with me, how it brought it all down to the basics of being healthy in the four main areas of life.

I also remember one by Noah Kagan more recently in which he listed the ways to make a blog post go viral, and then he actually had that blog post go viral.

WHAT ARE TEN YOU'VE READ
that you liked very much, and why?

1 _____

2 _____

3 _____

4 _____

5 _____

6 _____

7 _____

8 _____

9 _____

10 _____

❏ PHYSICAL   ❏ SPIRITUAL   ❏ EMOTIONAL

78) TEN THINGS YOU WOULD REALLY LIKE TO SEE HAPPENING IN YOUR LIFE WITHIN

THE NEXT YEAR, AND WHY?

I would like to see this book published and I would like people to use it and share their results with me. @ClaudiaYoga #ResultsIdeaMachine

Sometimes just listing the things we would like to see happening, even if we don't look at them ever again, can have a surprising effect on our subconscious.

We can write them, let them go, and let "other parts of our brain" get it done.

WHAT ARE TEN THINGS *you'd like to see happen for you?*

1 _____

2 _____

3 _____

4 _____

5 _____

6 _____

7 _____

8 _____

9 _____

10 _____

❏ PHYSICAL   ❏ SPIRITUAL   ❏ EMOTIONAL

79) Ten meals I could cook next week and the shopping list that goes together with it so I don't have to go to the supermarket at all.

If you don't cook in your house, then this is an especially helpful exercise as it has you thinking and getting out of your comfort zone.

If you do cook, I've found this exercise to be resourceful for me, because now, when we go somewhere for business and we rent a house, I already know, by heart, what to buy in the supermarket so I don't have to go get anything again. I don't do it for a week, but I have it down for up to 4 days.

For example, I like a dish James cooked for me the other day; it is fish, sole in particular, with lemon juice on top and pesto sauce. I garnish it with chopped carrots, zucchini, onions, garlic and other veggies. Everything goes in the oven.

30 minutes in the oven and it is done. Easy! So that could be one meal.

What are your ten?

1 _____

2 _____

3 _____

4 _____

5 _____

6 _____

7 _____

8 _____

9 _____

10 _____

❑ PHYSICAL   ❑ SPIRITUAL   ❑ EMOTIONAL

80) IF YOU COULD MAKE AN INTER-STELLAR, SILVER PLATE SHAPE, THAT WILL TRAVEL THROUGH THE UNIVERSE IN SEARCH OF OTHER LIFE, AND YOU COULD WRITE IN IT JUST THREE WORDS, IN ANY LANGUAGE, ENGLISH WILL DO, WHAT ARE THE THREE WORDS YOU WOULD WRITE?

You can go from humor to profound philosophical truths in three words. It does take some effort, but think… Someone in another galaxy will read them. What would you say?

I would say: Breathe. Kindness; Now.

Breath defines us a species, kindness is what I wish for in everyone, and now seems to be the only real thing to me.

SO, IN YOUR OWN CLOSE ENCOUNTER, *what are your three words?*

1 _____

2 _____

3 _____

4 _____

5 _____

6 _____

7 _____

8 _____

9 _____

10 _____

❑ PHYSICAL   ❑ SPIRITUAL   ❑ EMOTIONAL

81) Ten expressions we often use which may not necessarily mean what we think they mean, or which may not be appropriate:

Y̶ou know how sometimes we say "same difference"? When we really mean, "it makes no difference". Why do we do that? After all if it is the same difference then it is the same, and it does not mean that it makes no difference.

Or, when we say he/she "swept me off my feet". When I look at the words there I wonder... If I got swept of my feet I would probably fall and get hurt, which sometimes happens in relationships, but it may not be the intention of the expression.

Coming up with ten will be a challenge, but we are far into the book and we are already idea machines. Also, you could keep your note pad nearby and have it throughout the day.

What are ten expressions
you use that could be reflected upon?

1 _____

2 _____

3 _____

4 _____

5 _____

6 _____

7 _____

8 _____

9 _____

10 _____

❏ PHYSICAL   ❏ SPIRITUAL   ❏ EMOTIONAL

82) TEN IDEAS FOR *SELFIES* YOU COULD MAKE TODAY
THAT GIVE A PHILOSOPHICAL MESSAGE.

For example, if you were eating a sandwich with a begging person behind you on the streets of NY, and you took your phone out and a photo of yourself, that could be, even if over-done, a philosophical message behind a self portrait.

WHAT ARE OTHER TEN IDEAS?

1 _____

2 _____

3 _____

4 _____

5 _____

6 _____

7 _____

8 _____

9 _____

10 _____

❑ PHYSICAL   ❑ SPIRITUAL   ❑ EMOTIONAL

83) IDEA SEX: Look at the Ten People You Know but have not been in touch lately from a previous list (or come up with the ones you remember) and match them with THE QUALITIES THAT YOU ADMIRE FROM PEOPLE YOU LISTED IN ANOTHER IDEA DAY, ON WHICH YOU MENTIONED "WHAT THEY ARE ALL ABOUT".

Do the people you know match any of these qualities?

I said 'my uncle' for the people I know, and 'Tony Robbins' for people I admire. When I look into it I see that they both stand up for their own truths, and that they want to help others by showing them the way. For example my uncle took me to see a production of "A Doll's House" when I was very young, and it caused a deep impression of me. Tony Robbins's books have always inspired me to think big, and to think 'how can I help'.

So both of them, in their own way, are inspirations to me.

Now it is time for you to have idea sex:

1 _____

2 _____

3 _____

4 _____

5 _____

6 _____

7 _____

8 _____

9 _____

10 _____

❏ PHYSICAL   ❏ SPIRITUAL   ❏ EMOTIONAL

84) List ten things that you have learned, or gained, or re-directed, or thought deeply about, because you have been working on your idea muscle this long.

One thing that became clear to me as I practiced listing ideas is that when the mind is active there is very little chance that I can calm it down and focus.

However, if I put it to work, especially when it is over-heated and ready to complaint or take me down and drain me, then the work itself focuses her. Meaning that I get to use the energy that could hurt me, and put it in the service of coming up with ideas that might help myself, or others.

I find that when the idea muscle sweats it's like a workout. Later on my mind is not so prone to just go off a cliff. And I get to be more focused.

I would like to hear what you have learned, so please tweet to me @ClaudiaYoga #IdeaMuscleInsights

What are your ten insights?

1 _____

2 _____

3 _____

4 _____

5 _____

6 _____

7 _____

8 _____

9 _____

10 _____

☐ PHYSICAL   ☐ SPIRITUAL   ☐ EMOTIONAL

85) Ten things I would like
to do before I die.

I know I want to see the temples in Japan, and I also want to see where inspiration takes me when it comes to my yoga practice. One thing in my bucket list has always been to meet and marry someone I loved deeply who would love me back.

Having such list made me aware of what I needed to focus on, and what we focus on expands, I am lucky to be married to James.

What are ten things *you would like to do*
or experience before you die?

1 _____

2 _____

3 _____

4 _____

5 _____

6 _____

7
_____

8
_____

9
_____

10
_____

❏ PHYSICAL   ❏ SPIRITUAL   ❏ EMOTIONAL

86) Sometimes we get on a "funk". List ten things you could do next time this awful mood strikes to get out of it.

~

For me taking a walk (when it is not freezing outside) works very well, or talking to a friend or emailing even. As long as I can keep it real and say what is troubling me.

Usually it is a combination of things that help me in getting out, and sometimes nothing works, and I just need to live through the day, one day at the time.

What are ten things you could do if
this mood was to strike to get out of it?

1 _____

2 _____

3 _____

4 _____

5 _____

6 _____

7 _____

8 _____

9 _____

10 _____

☐ PHYSICAL   ☐ SPIRITUAL   ☐ EMOTIONAL

87) Ten Dreams I Remember From My life
and roughly what they were about.

~~

If you never dream then you can make some up, or come up with your own list of other things to list.

I do remember dreams; I have one from when I was 7 in which I saw a lamp. That is the dream. Nothing else. A lamp.

Thing is this lamp evoked a feeling. It was a feeling of not being safe. It was indicating that something was upsetting in the air. That dream has stayed with me.

Sometimes our subconscious talks to us through dreams by mixing and matching things from waking life and re-arranging them in strange ways.

What are ten things you remember
and what were they about?

1 _____

2 _____

3 _____

4 _____

5 _____

6 _____

7 _____

8 _____

9 _____

10 _____

☐ PHYSICAL   ☐ SPIRITUAL   ☐ EMOTIONAL

88) Ten "stream of consciousness" PARAGRAPHS

Use the two words "start now" and then write a whole sentence. Then when you finish that sentence write "start now" again and write another paragraph. Repeat it ten times.

This exercise is based on May Sarton's work. And it gets me every time. I never know where it will take me.

Remember to keep it to one paragraph, but do it at your own risk, because it may inspire you to keep writing.

Tweet to me if you get one you really like @ClaudiaYoga #IdeaMuscleNow.

For me it goes something like this:

Start now, I am overlooking one of the greatest cities in the world and the gold of that building on 30th street matches perfectly the silver tone of the Freedom tower.

Now you, go:

1. Start now…

2. Start now…

3. Start now…

4. Start now…

214

5. Start now...

_____

6. Start now...

_____

7. Start now...

_____

8. Start now...

_____

9. Start now...

_____

10. Start now...

_____

☐ PHYSICAL ☐ SPIRITUAL ☐ EMOTIONAL

89) LIST TEN WAYS IN WHICH YOU COULD IMPROVE YOUR LIFE BY 1% THIS MONTH. YOU DON'T HAVE TO ACT ON IT, JUST LIST IT:

I know I could improve my life by 1% by sitting in silence a little longer in the mornings, say, three more minutes.

There is a difference in the quality of my awareness during the day when I get to sit for a long time in the morning.

WHAT ARE TEN WAYS *you can think of that would improve your life by just 1% this month:*

1 _____

2 _____

3 _____

4 _____

5 _____

6 _____

7 _____

8 _____

9 _____

10 _____

❑ PHYSICAL   ❑ SPIRITUAL   ❑ EMOTIONAL

90) AS A SPECIES WE ARE ALWAYS LOOKING FOR "NEW FRONTIERS". WE NEED NEW QUESTS, NEW TERRITORY, NEW VENTURES, JOURNEYS, AND EXPLORATIONS. WHAT ARE TEN NEW FRONTIERS YOU SEE FOR YOURSELF?

I want to write a book on how yoga transformed me because I recently wrote an article for the New York Observer and realized the feedback was pointing towards a need to find relief in different ways. I also want to do a podcast that is worth listening to, with great guests, because I love talking to people in down-to-earth terms, and I feel that the yoga community can get caught in fluff sometimes. These are some of my new frontiers. And by the day, because of the list making I come up with new frontiers.

Whenever we reach a milestone in our lives we get happy for a moment. But then, we just can't help it, being human makes us want the next release of dopamine, or, as Loretta Graziano Breuning puts it in her great book: *Meet Your Happy Chemicals*: "The great feeling that motivates the body to invest effort in pursuit."

SO WHAT ARE THE 10 *new frontiers you see for yourself, and why?*

1 _____

2 _____

3 _____

4 _____

5 _____

6 _____

7 _____

8 _____

9 _____

10 _____

❏ PHYSICAL   ❏ SPIRITUAL   ❏ EMOTIONAL

THE 90-DAY MARK
YOU'VE DONE NINETY DAYS
WORTH OF IDEAS NOW.

CONGRATULATIONS.

I want to pause for a minute and acknowledge your work and determination. That was not easy. And you did it. Pat yourself on the back. I also do a little dance when I mark milestones, and Tweet and Facebook it. But you can do your own ritual.

You are now well on the way to transforming your life in magical ways. Or maybe it's already begun to happen?

And of course, now is time to *up the game.*

Sir John Templeton, a billionaire and possibly one of the greatest investors of last century said it better than I could:

"Don't try to be a go getter. Try to be a go giver."

And so now it is time to give.

TIME TO GIVE

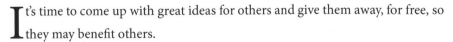

It's time to come up with great ideas for others and give them away, for free, so they may benefit others.

It is now time to go from ambition to meaning. From the small universe of what I can do for me, to the meaningful universe-at-large of how can I help?

From now on we are going to expand the reach of the idea machine and dip our toes into the waters of what happens when our ideas are for others.

This is the key to abundance. The door opens with the first list.

How do I
Give The Ideas Away?

Since your idea muscle is in great shape by now, it might be that some of the lists you write contain pretty substantial ideas.

If this is the case you may be tempted to send them, share them, and see them flourish into manifestation. That is a great thing, trust your instincts and go for it.

We get many questions when it comes to how to send them, for example:

IS THERE A STRUCTURE TO FOLLOW WHEN SENDING IDEAS AWAY?

The important detail is to *personalize* the emails. So the only structure should be personalization. Make sure to show that these are not just ideas you came up lightly, show the specialized effort that went into creating them for a specific case, but don't boast.

For example, when someone says: "I'd like to help you and so I came up with these ten ideas for you", that line is clearly about them, not about the person receiving the ideas. It is serving the person who is sending them, glorifying them or making them feel good.

If instead someone was to say, "I noticed that you are looking for alternative titles for your book and since it is about "ideas" I thought of these ten that reflect not only your work but also the message of hour previous books", then something else is at work. I can already see that they mean to talk about something that is important to the receiver and that they have put work into it, not just ideas on the fly.

The person receiving the ideas can tell right away whether the person sending them has put a lot of thought into helping and making the ideas coherent with the work. And that is what will determine if they will read them.

How Do I Finish An Email In Which I Offer Ideas?

Remember that we are giving away the ideas for *free*.

I would make sure to reinforce that there are ZERO strings attached and that we expect nothing in return.

If we add at the end that we have been working on this website for a long time and we offer a product that is very valuable, and on and on, then we are missing the point.

Giving ideas away freely means exactly that. It means we are idea machines and so we trust the flow of ideas and we know they return in the form of abundance. We just don't know what form that will be, but we don't care. It is the principle underneath that we are testing.

The form that it might take could be a connection, a new influential friend, an invitation to collaborate, an invitation to come over and talk, or nothing. And we need to be ready for all of those options, including nothing.

Complete trust means we just offer them and say: "use them". And we say nothing else. We don't point to a website or a crow-funding project or a video or anything. We just offer the ideas and let it be.

This is what distinguishes an idea machine from an idea producer.

An idea producer wants something out of it; an idea machine knows that being abundant in ideas means being abundant, period.

I have zero expectations of you giving me anything in return for this book. In fact I will try to distribute it at the lowest cost I can, as I follow the Amazon guidelines. I am not in it for the money; I am in it for the love of ideas. And by the time you read it I will probably have a couple of months or years of 10-ideas-a-day under my belt. Maybe I will be an atomic idea machine, who knows?

So make sure that when you give your ideas away, especially the good ones, the ones you cherish, you do it like a pro. You mean it. You trust the wealth that is in your idea muscle, you are not hoarding, and you are willing to share.

Someone wrote to James recently saying she had a brilliant idea for LinkedIn but she did not want to just give it and then see it happen and get no credit.

We made a whole Ask Altucher (episode 45) just to answer that, and the short answer is: GIVE THEM AWAY. Leave the fear behind.

For starters, LinkedIn may not even look at your idea. You could be sending it to the wrong person, or the person may be in a bad mood, or whatever. A million things can happen.

And if the idea is picked up and taken upon, then who knows?

James sent ideas to Amazon and they invited him to Seattle, to their head-quarters, and not once, but twice!

If your ideas are really good, then people might in all likelihood want to talk to you.

If you hoard them for fear that they will be used without you getting credit then you are still thinking small, and not trusting the process. Nothing wrong with being there, but it is a good indicator of where you are.

I have full trust that if you've been writing ten ideas a day for this long, and you are reading this now, then your idea muscle is toned and you don't feel like hoarding anymore.

You've probably seen the ideas work in your life, in difficult situations. You've seen the power of looking at alternatives quickly, coming up with solutions on the go, offering alternatives. You feel it.

You are probably already thinking in different ways and helping those around you most of the time.

It's time to think bigger now, so let's go.

BECOME AN IDEA MACHINE

MACHINE
BECAUSE IDEAS ARE
THE CURRENCY OF THE 21ST CENTURY

CLAUDIA
AZULA ALTUCHER

PART TWO:

90 MORE DAYS

91) Ten Business From The Area That I Live In That Will Probably Go Bankrupt And Why?

⌒

You can tell when a business is trying hard and when one is not. You can even see the writing on the wall when one is about to go out of business.

For example, there was a shop on the main street here where I live called "Dolls and Balls". I kid you not. That is what they sold. Balls (basketballs, footballs, pool balls), and dolls (creepy old dolls, new dolls).

Regardless of how artistic a town considers itself, my guess is there is a limit. Now I confess I only heard of this store, never even saw it. But there is another place in the next town where I order my breakfast and I get it an hour later. Always. I would guess that will be counterproductive, and the reason why is because I'm hungry and don't want to wait so long. If I could make a suggestion to this place it would be to not take so long. And if I could be in the kitchen for a morning maybe I could help streamline the process or at least come up with ten further ideas.

So list ten business *in your area that you see are hurting, and why? What could they do different?*

1 _____

2 _____

3 _____

4 _____

5 _____

6 _____

7 _____

8 _____

9 _____

10 _____

☐ PHYSICAL   ☐ SPIRITUAL   ☐ EMOTIONAL

92) Pick one of the businesses from yesterday and decide you are the 'Marcus Lemonis', or the consultant that will help them thrive. What are your ten ideas?

Marcus Lemonis, from the CNBC show *The Profit*, goes into businesses that are in trouble and reviews their people, their processes, and their product. His objective, of course, is to make the profitable.

If one of them has fallen off the wagon, he helps, either by putting money, remodeling, giving advice, and/or even cleaning toilets. He does whatever is necessary.

So pick a business *that is dear to you from the list you wrote yesterday and come up with ten ideas of what they could do to stay in business and thrive:*

1 _____

2 _____

3 _____

4 _____

5 _____

6 _____

7 _____

8 _____

9 _____

10 _____

❑ PHYSICAL　❑ SPIRITUAL　❑ EMOTIONAL

93) 10 Book Titles That Would Make The *New York Times* Best Seller List just by the power of the title.

OK, nobody can guarantee the *New York Times* Best Seller list, but who cares? Well, maybe one person can, that would be Michael Drew, and you can hear the 30-minute podcast James and I did with him on AskAltucher.com (Episode 105). Michael has put 100% of the books he works on within the prestigious list, and he spills the beans on that show.

But we can still come up with best selling wanna-be titles. How about *"Gut Brain"*. Wouldn't you want to read a book with that title?

After all, all the others did great, right? *Grain Brain, Wheat Belly,* why not *"gut" brain*? – And what is the book about? It's about how there are lots of neurochemicals in our gut and our brain makes decisions from there as much as the other brain. That is why we have *gut feelings.* Oh I feel the impetus towards writing… Must finish this book first.

What are ten titles *you can think of,*
and what are they about?

1 _____

2 _____

3 _____

4 _____

5 _____

6 _____

7 _____

8 _____

9 _____

10 _____

◻ PHYSICAL   ◻ SPIRITUAL   ◻ EMOTIONAL

94) Ten Weekend Workshops Ideas You Could Offer in Your Local Community Town Hall

~~

We all have something to teach. Even if you are seventeen you probably know something, like how to use computers, or what are some cool words that the younger generations use these days?

I could offer a workshop on coming up with ideas. I would call it "Idea Sex For Money".

It would last 2 to 3 hours and it would be highly interactive. People would exchange ideas, and then they would choose one and come up with further ideas. Nobody would be allowed to put anyone down. We would all cherish all ideas, even the ones we don't like, because there is no such thing as a bad idea. Bad ideas are just the bed on which the good ones lie.

What are your ten workshops? *What are they about? How long is the class? What would people do? Answer all four questions for all ten ideas.*

Tweet to me your favorite please @ClaudiaYoga #IdeaMachineWorkshop

1 _____

2 _____

3 _____

4 _____

5 _____

6 _____

7 _____

8 _____

9 _____

10 _____

☐ PHYSICAL   ☐ SPIRITUAL   ☐ EMOTIONAL

95) TEN BUSINESSES THAT COULD BENEFIT FROM MERGING ALL THEIR EFFORTS AND CREATING A MONOPOLY.

I see a new yoga blog come on line every day. Then there are the printed magazines, then there are aggregators. There is a lot of content all over the web.

I wonder if they were all to merge into one and use their massive collective social media reach to say we are all one now, and you can find everything here.

Would it work? I don't know. Some people who know a lot more than me seem to think yes.

WHAT ARE TEN THAT YOU CAN THINK OF?

1 _____

2 _____

3 _____

4 _____

5 _____

6 _____

7 _____

8 _____

9 _____

10 _____

☐ PHYSICAL   ☐ SPIRITUAL   ☐ EMOTIONAL

96) 10 Articles You Can Write That Can Make A difference

F or example: 10 ways in which taking out the garbage helped my relationship is one idea I just had.

Nobody wants to take out the garbage out. And yet, doing that little bit of work can mean a lot for a stressed out partner.

What are your ten ideas?

1 _____

2 _____

3 _____

4 _____

5 _____

6 _____

7 _____

8 _____

9 _____

10 _____

☐ PHYSICAL   ☐ SPIRITUAL   ☐ EMOTIONAL

97) 10 SHORT WORKOUT ROUTINES TO TARGET DIFFERENT AREAS OF THE BODY THAT PEOPLE CAN DO IN UNDER 10 MINUTES IN THE OFFICE AND WHILE NOBODY IS WATCHING

If you are not into fitness don't worry because as you come up with ideas you can include things that you do, for example to de-stress, and as you keep going you may notice that just taking a walk helps.

For me the best thing is to stand up every hour and stretch the front of my body. I do this by putting my hands on my waist and leaning backwards, breathing there for one or two counts and then inhaling as I come up. And by the way, the 'inhaling as I come up' is the key tip, it comes from yoga, I get emails about it, it is THAT important.

The front of the body never gets a stretch because we are always curved down over our desks, and this simple exercise helps decompress the front of the body. That is one idea.

WHAT ARE YOUR TEN?

1 _____

2 _____

3 _____

4 _____

5 _____

6 _____

7 _____

8 _____

9 _____

10 _____

☐ PHYSICAL   ☐ SPIRITUAL   ☐ EMOTIONAL

98) How to ruin your relationship in 10 steps, and why is it that these ten things are so harmful?

Looking at relationships (with your significant other or your boss or your child) in this way is challenging and different. It can even be scary.

However it points out to the big "no-nos", and that is always helpful.

I know that if I get cranky and start complaining that turns James away from me. He can go into his man cave and it can take a full day to recover trust and to establish good lines of communication.

So whenever I find myself all upset I find other ways to cope. I still share with James how I am feeling but in the heat of the anger I use tools like friends I can call, or writing, or even walking and breathing to re-charge and not put it all on my partner.

So what does your list look like?

1 _____

2 _____

3 _____

4 _____

5 _____

6 _____

7 _____

8 _____

9 _____

10 _____

☐ **PHYSICAL**　　☐ **SPIRITUAL**　　☐ **EMOTIONAL**

99) 10 DOCUMENTARIES YOU

RECOMMEND WATCHING AND WHY?

I enjoyed a documentary by Tom Shadyac called *"I Am"*. In it he poses two questions: 1) what is wrong with our world and 2) what can we do to help.

Within it he has a lot of scenes that show how the way we live can be unsustainable if we do not wake up to the fact that we are not what we think we are.

I believe that awakening is important to all of us, now, and that is why I like it.

WHAT ARE YOUR TEN?

1 _____

2 _____

3 _____

4 _____

5 _____

6 _____

7 _____

8 _____

9 _____

10 _____

☐ PHYSICAL   ☐ SPIRITUAL   ☐ EMOTIONAL

100) 10 TED TALK
IDEAS YOU COULD GIVE

T ED talks are very specific, they need to have a topic that will feel new, even if it isn't, they must contain innovative ideas and they have to contain ideas worth spreading.

And that is just some of the requirements that I read on James prep-sheet when he was getting ready for his own TEDX in San Diego in late 2014.

As far as I can see, any old topic can be turned into a TED talk as long as it has a new and interesting twist. Which, by the way qualifies it as *idea sex*. The possibilities are endless.

For example, I like movies with deep philosophical backbones, like Star Wars, and I also like entrepreneurship. One idea I have is to merge the ancient philosophy of that epic set of movies with day-to-day business.

And as you can imagine, that talk would include the Tao of the daily listing of ten ideas as a way to "train" the mind. This book (not me) would be a Yoda of sorts guiding and keeping us sharp, not trusting all other senses so much, and just focusing the mind.

WHAT ARE YOUR TEN? *Why are they interesting?*
What is the twist?

1 _____

2 _____

3
_____

4
_____

5
_____

6
_____

7
_____

8
_____

9
_____

10
_____

☐ PHYSICAL   ☐ SPIRITUAL   ☐ EMOTIONAL

101) 10 IDEAS FOR SHORT YOUTUBE VIDEOS I CAN MAKE THAT TEACH SOMETHING.

We can pretty much ask YouTube anything and get an answer, sometimes in under 2 minutes.

James wants to do short, 2-minute videos every day that answer questions like: What is the Federal Reserve? Or what is a bank? I am taking him up on that. I love the idea.

I've made some videos already in which I talk about how to open the hips, from a yoga point of view. And I continue to answer questions I get in video form; in fact I created a new site called PortableYoga.com where I have a page dedicate to video answers.

The world needs answers; otherwise YouTube would not be the 3rd search engine in the world (after Google and Bing)

WHAT ARE TEN YOU COULD DO?

1 _____

2 _____

3 _____

4 _____

5 _____

6 _____

7 _____

8 _____

9 _____

10 _____

❑ PHYSICAL   ❑ SPIRITUAL   ❑ EMOTIONAL

102) 10 books I Could Write Today, Under 40 Pages That Give Value.

R ecently, while was preparing for a workshop on yoga to prevent back pain, I read three books that look at alternative ways of facing and treating it. The books recommended better breathing, better posture, and an understanding of deep, and perhaps repressed emotions.

The exercises in those books had a lot of common with many of the yoga asanas that I already teach, and so it was delightful to put them together in a preventive yoga sequence (which by the way, can now also be found on that PortableYoga.com site).

Knowing what I know now, including the questions that I received from participants of the workshop would make for a nice 40-page booklet (12,000 to 15,000 words).

IF YOU ARE BRAVE AND DARE, *go ahead and pick one of your ten, write it and publish. Go to kindle direct and figure it out, you are an Idea machine after all. Bonus points if you upload it to Amazon. Let me know* @ClaudiaYoga #IdeaMachineSelfPublished

1 _____

2 _____

3 _____

248

4 _____

5 _____

6 _____

7 _____

8 _____

9 _____

10 _____

☐ PHYSICAL   ☐ SPIRITUAL   ☐ EMOTIONAL

103) 10 WORLD PROBLEMS THAT CAN BE SOLVED BY TECHNOLOGY AND WHAT IS THE NEXT STEP

E very time I visit Buenos Aires I am struck by how much people complain about insecurity, about roberies and so on. There is a lot of poverty in Buenos Aires, and I hope things get better, but so far it has not happened.

I wonder if there was an app where people would assign five friends or family members that would be on watch and so whenever in doubt, at the touch of a button these five people would be alerted and hopefully one of them would take action to help.

Enlisting others is a viable idea to create safety, just like we have neighborhood watch in the United States, we could have it in Buenos Aires as well, only this would be virtual.

THE NEXT STEP WOULD BE TO SPECK IT OUT *and hire a designer while immersing myself in security technology, of which I don't know much. Maybe not a good idea for me, but hey! It's an idea. What are your ten?*

1 _____

2 _____

3 _____

4 _____

5 _____

6 _____

7 _____

8 _____

9 _____

10 _____

☐ PHYSICAL　　☐ SPIRITUAL　　☐ EMOTIONAL

104) 10 Suggestions For A
Celebrity To Reinvent

$\sim$

My stepdaughters and James are fans of Lindsay Lohan, and through them I've come to see her work. I see how talented she is and it's painful to see how her personal life plays against her.

I would have to think long and hard before giving a much younger woman any advise, but I am pretending, for the purposes of this exercise, that this celebrity actually wants it and that I want to help.

I would suggest to Lindsay to start listing ten ideas a day on how her life could be more fun for her and also for her fans. For example, if she was to reinvent herself and produce a movie that focuses on issues like the ones she has battled with because of her upbringing, early fame, etc. Or, another idea could be a documentary about celebrities who went through drug-hell and came out of it.

What is the celebrity that needs *your help* *and what are your ten ideas for him or her?*

1 _____

2 _____

3 _____

4 _____

5 _____

6 _____

7 _____

8 _____

9 _____

10 _____

☐ PHYSICAL   ☐ SPIRITUAL   ☐ EMOTIONAL

105) 10 Historical moments that could be turned into soap operas like Downton Abbey

There was a movie that caused a big impression on me when I was very young. It was set in the 1850's, in a very conservative Buenos Aires, whereby one girl of high society fell in love with a priest who also had connections (he was the nephew of one of the northern province's governor). They fell deeply in love and escaped together but did not make it far before they were captured and killed by government forces.

It is a sad story but it gave me a glimpse into another time and a country that was the place where I was born but in a time I knew nothing about. And I would like to see this turned into episodes because there is high stakes and lots of drama.

WHAT ARE YOUR 10 *historical moments that you could turn into a TV show?*

1 _____

2 _____

3 _____

4 _____

5 _____

6 _____

7 _____

8 _____

9 _____

10 _____

☐ PHYSICAL ☐ SPIRITUAL ☐ EMOTIONAL

106) 10 Suggestions To Make Weddings Fun, Special, and Under 10K

W e all know how expensive weddings can be, but there is a lot that is tied into it because of tradition and expectations.

What I propose is that we look at weddings as entrepreneurs and offer the same values and traditions but for a whole less money.

One idea I have is to make the event virtual. Where only family and the very close friends of the groom and bride will be present, hence keeping the cost of venue and food low, and have the party open to everyone who wants to attend through Skype.

People can leave Skype videos (which can be recorded for the future), and take photos with the bride and groom virtually, making the whole wedding a lot more interactive and not so static. A facilitator would make things flow.

Another idea is to get married "my style" which is let everyone know that the event is at city hall tomorrow morning and anyone who is around is welcome to come over for the ceremony and lunch, but nobody is obliged. I'm aware that is not to everyone's taste though, good thing it's your turn to come up with ten ideas now.

WHAT ARE YOUR TEN?

1 _____

2 _____

3

_____

4

_____

5

_____

6

_____

7

_____

8

_____

9

_____

10

_____

◻ **PHYSICAL**   ◻ **SPIRITUAL**   ◻ **EMOTIONAL**

107) 10 Hotels You
Would Love To Visit Because...

The hotels you are about to list do not have to exist already; they can, and likely will be, in your imagination.

I heard of a hotel in the Maldives that is totally underwater, and although it makes me feel claustrophobic I have to say the view from the rooms sounds interesting.

How about those new hotel rooms that are just small boxes? I believe they exist in the some airports in Japan so you can get a night sleep while you wait for your connection without the expense of a full room.

WHAT ARE TEN OTHER IDEAS *for special, out of the box hotels?*
And why is it you would visit them, what makes them special?

1 _____

2 _____

3 _____

4 _____

5 _____

6 _____

7 _____

8 _____

9 _____

10 _____

❏ PHYSICAL ❏ SPIRITUAL ❏ EMOTIONAL

108) TODAY, FIND TEN EMAIL CONVERSATIONS FROM FIVE YEARS AGO, THEN CONTINUE THE CONVERSATION.

5 years ago I was corresponding to a friend of mine that had also been fired from the corporate, safe job.

We were talking about what our plans were and how we would make ends meet and so on.

A few weeks ago I took the email again as if nothing, and continued the conversation.

It took a few days as she had changed emails but she did respond, and a friendship was re-kindled.

WHAT ARE TEN PEOPLE *you were talking to five years ago?*

1 _____

2 _____

3 _____

4 _____

5 _____

6 _____

7 _____

8 _____

9 _____

10 _____

☐ PHYSICAL   ☐ SPIRITUAL   ☐ EMOTIONAL

109) Ten Things I Learned From
This Amazing Teacher

W hen I first came to New York City I took classes at an acting studio because they gave me a student visa, which allowed me to work part-time and hence stay in the USA.

Under these unlikely circumstances I met an extraordinary dance teacher called Mary Anthony. She was the personification of grace and efficiency, and she would always repeat: "be aware of the self, not self-aware".

I remember her classes even today, 16 years later. And one of the exercises I teach that include drumming with breathing comes directly from her. That is the type of impact she had on me.

What are the ten things you learned *from that amazing teacher you are thinking of? Bonus points if you share with all of us in a blog or podcast so we can all learn, let me know @ClaudiaYoga #IdeaMachine10ThingsILearned*

1 _____

2 _____

3 _____

4 _____

5 _____

6 _____

7 _____

8 _____

9 _____

10 _____

    ☐ PHYSICAL   ☐ SPIRITUAL   ☐ EMOTIONAL

110) AMERICAN AIRLINES WANTS A NEW NAME FOR ITS BRAND

A merican Airlines has merged and gone bankrupt more times than we care to remember. They seem to transform themselves yearly, but their name never changes.

This is a hypothetical case in which they are thinking of re-branding completely and changing name and they want you to give them ten ideas.

They need it to be no more than two words, of course, and they want it to reflect innovation, and working together.

"American Universe" is the name that comes to me. Something that reflects the future, and how high they are going. It is also a pretty arrogant name but then again, why not take over the whole thing? Someone is going to…

WHAT ARE YOUR TEN IDEAS *for names for them?*

1 _____

2 _____

3 _____

4 _____

5 _____

6 _____

7 _____

8 _____

9 _____

10 _____

❏ PHYSICAL   ❏ SPIRITUAL   ❏ EMOTIONAL

111) SELECT A FRIEND YOU KNOW WHO IS STRUGGLING RIGHT NOW. THEN WRITE TEN ACTIONABLE, EASY IDEAS THAT CAN HELP THEM TODAY

James tells me that before he sent ten ideas to Jim Cramer about articles he could write he thought of them and streamlined them for months. By the time the ideas hit Cramer's inbox they were on fire, Jim wanted the articles written pronto! And he wanted James to write them.

As an idea machine you can now help others in a significant way. For example, I have a friend who is travelling and who wanted to say thank you to a teacher she had just gotten to know and whom she admired very much. As soon as I heard her saying that I got the idea that she could interview her so that others would get to know this teacher and how good she is.

My friend embraced the idea and her recording is now one of the episodes in my yoga podcast, which we ended producing together.

SO WHAT IS ONE FRIEND *you could help today and what are ten, good ideas for him or her?*

1 _____

2 _____

3 _____

4 _____

5 _____

6 _____

7 _____

8 _____

9 _____

10 _____

☐ PHYSICAL ☐ SPIRITUAL ☐ EMOTIONAL

112) 10 Crazy Things You Did, That Were Completely Out of Your Comfort Zone And
What You Learned From Them?

Coming to the United States with no money and no connections was the craziest, most naïve thing I did in my life. But If I was in my early 20's I would do it all over again.

Living in a foreign country was at first intimidating, brutal, confusing and scary. But I learned to clear the way and make a life for myself and with that came some skill. For example, I had to learn to make people like me even though, at first, I did not speak their language very well.

For the first year of my stay in the United States I smiled a whole lot, just so that people would keep on talking to me. That is how I found new opportunities. Eventually I did learn the language in full, which came handy.

But it does not have to be that crazy. It can also be leaving a job behind because you did not like it, and what did you learn?

What is in your list of ten?

1 _____

2 _____

3 _____

4 _____

5 _____

6 _____

7 _____

8 _____

9 _____

10 _____

☐ PHYSICAL   ☐ SPIRITUAL   ☐ EMOTIONAL

113) HOW DO YOU COPE WITH ANXIETY?

Provide us with ten suggestions we can use, that work for you (not from what doctors say) to help those moments where adrenaline starts shooting and we can't control our fears.

For me it helps to talk to someone I love and respect like James, or to take a walk and drink chamomile tea, or to journal, to just start writing about it and not stop until when I calm down.

What are your ten suggestions?

IF YOU HAVE TEN GOOD ONES *and you publish them*
let me know @ClaudiaYoga #IdeaMachine10AntiStress

1 _____

2 _____

3 _____

4 _____

5 _____

6 _____

7 _____

8 _____

9 _____

10 _____

☐ PHYSICAL   ☐ SPIRITUAL   ☐ EMOTIONAL

114) IDEA SEX: WRITE AN ARTICLE ABOUT SOME-THING YOU ARE INTERESTED IN, MAKE IT GOOD BY

TELLING A STORY AROUND IT.

~~

Send it to 10 different online publications. If you are already a writer then up the game. Try to get published by the *New York Times*, or *Cracked*.

If you have never done this before then the list is somewhat easier.

You probably already have an idea for a good article from the day in which you wrote topics for your 40-page booklet.

So now you can write an article, which is a lot shorter than 40 pages and can be done in fewer than 2000 words.

The point of the exercise is to get it distributed in a venue where you've never been published before. It is a dare, and also writing and a sharing of value. It is a triple *Idea Machine* exercise.

If you do get it published let me know… You know the drill.

WHAT ARE THE TEN IDEAS

for the article you are going to write?

1 _____

2 _____

3 _____

4 _____

5 _____

6 _____

7 _____

8 _____

9 _____

10 _____

☐ PHYSICAL   ☐ SPIRITUAL   ☐ EMOTIONAL

115)10 Business That Could Be Built On Top Of LinkedIn

M ost people use LinkedIn. It is the social network for professionals and for the workforce.

One business I could see built on top of it is conferences.

For example, gathering the interests of certain groups, and then creating a web event, sponsored and integrated with invitations to influencers and the public in general.

Another business could be a teaching platform that would search for open jobs and pair them with videos that offer interview tips for those specific positions or industries.

WHAT ARE YOUR TEN IDEAS? *Send them to LinkedIn if you like them. Remember that ideas spread like currency. Don't hoard them, let them go out and see the light of day.*

1 _____

2 _____

3 _____

4 _____

5 _____

6 _____

7 _____

8 _____

9 _____

10 _____

☐ **PHYSICAL**   ☐ **SPIRITUAL**   ☐ **EMOTIONAL**

116) 10 Ideas for the major of your town that would improve tourism and flow of people so that businesses in the area thrive.

Ilive in a small town and I think we could benefit enormously if right on the train station there were pamphlets or a bar code that people could scan to get all the information from the area.

There are lots of things to do in every single block up and down the main street but without one place where all the information can be centralized it is hard to find.

For example many hikers come here during the weekend but not many know that there are great yoga classes in the studio that is on the third floor, one block from the train.

An app or even a pamphlet with information would help all the local businesses and also the people coming to see the town.

What are your ten ideas?

1 _____

2 _____

3 _____

4 _____

5 _____

6 _____

7 _____

8 _____

9 _____

10 _____

☐ PHYSICAL ☐ SPIRITUAL ☐ EMOTIONAL

117) 10 Suggestions for Outer Space tourism that Richard Branson could use.

⌐⌐

Even if I had the enormous amount of money it takes to go to outer space whenever the first ship is ready I don't think I would.

It is too scary for me and I like keeping my feet on the earth.

So I have another suggestions, like for example, for a fraction of the cost take me, or anyone who is scared of going out there, on a plane that can offer the no gravity experience.

What are your ten ideas for him?

1 _____

2 _____

3 _____

4 _____

5 _____

6 _____

7 _____

8 _____

9 _____

10 _____

☐ PHYSICAL ☐ SPIRITUAL ☐ EMOTIONAL

118) 10 Things I could do to generate an extra 300 dollars this week.

⌐

An idea machine cannot shy away from this. But note that savings or not spending would not do it because that would be keeping money rather than "generating".

To generate money a service or a product needs to be exchanged.

For example I could grab that 40-page report we talked about in a previous list and sell it.

Back pain, which was the topic of my booklet, costs us almost 90 billion dollars a year so there must be a market foo preventing it.

What are your ten ideas?

1 _____

2 _____

3 _____

4 _____

5 _____

6 _____

7 _____

8 _____

9 _____

10 _____

☐ PHYSICAL   ☐ SPIRITUAL   ☐ EMOTIONAL

119) 10 Body/Mind Hacks You Learned
In The Past 12 Months

It can be anything from a better way to eat or to sleep or to travel. It can be a habit modification, anything you learned or incorporated into your routine that made things better for you and that you learned in the past 12 months.

One thing I've learned and incorporated into my bedroom is black out curtains, because the slightest amount of light can be absorbed not just by the eyes, but the skin, which is the largest organ we have. I learned this by reading Tucker Max's book *How To Naturally Increase Testosterone* and I have to say, the black out curtains work for me.

WHAT ARE TEN *that worked for you?*

1 _____

2 _____

3 _____

4 _____

5 _____

6 _____

7 _____

8 _____

9 _____

10 _____

❑ PHYSICAL   ❑ SPIRITUAL   ❑ EMOTIONAL

.

120) 10 Products You Love
And Can Review

⌒

Reviews are good for everyone, especially when we find a product that works for us. I always recommend books I read that make a difference for me, as well as products.

What are ten products *or books you have used recently and what is one thing you could say about them that helped you while writing a review?*

1 _____

2 _____

3 _____

4 _____

5 _____

6 _____

7 _____

8 _____

9 _____

10 _____

☐ PHYSICAL   ☐ SPIRITUAL   ☐ EMOTIONAL

121) 10 Things You Wish You Knew When You Were Fifteen

It would have been helpful for me to know that the world was not as black as white, "follow the rules and you will be rewarded" as I thought it was back then.

There are other things. For example I grew up not trusting men because of examples I saw around me.

I wish someone had written a list of ten things that helped them, i.e.: I wish I could have read the ten things YOU wish you knew when you were 15.

So when you do, tweet me @ClaudiaYoga and do the hash-tag #IdeaMachineWishIKnew15

1 _____

2 _____

3 _____

4 _____

5 _____

6 _____

7 _____

8 _____

9 _____

10 _____

☐ PHYSICAL   ☐ SPIRITUAL   ☐ EMOTIONAL

122) 10 Relationships that could use a talk

$$\backsim$$

Find ten relationships in your life that could benefit from a heart to heart. It does not mean you have to actually do it, it just means you are going to think about these ten people and list an idea of how you could approach a conversation with them to express how their behavior or actions make you feel.

For example I have not spoken to a member of my family in a long time because the relationship became really toxic. I wish I could approach it in a balanced way, admitting the places where I went and continue to go wrong, but I also wish I would be heard. I wish I could tell this person that I never really meant any harm.

Who are your ten people? *And remember, it does not have to be very deep, it could be something simple like a neighbor playing loud music and what would be one way to approach a conversation in a meaningful and useful way.*

1 _____

2 _____

3 _____

4 _____

5 _____

6 _____

7 _____

8 _____

9 _____

10 _____

☐ **PHYSICAL**   ☐ **SPIRITUAL**   ☐ **EMOTIONAL**

123) Secret Helper: 10 Ways To Help
Today Without Taking Credit

You will probably come across situations throughout the day or even the week where you know you can help. The challenge is to list ways in which you could do it without taking credit or even being noticed.

For example, I know that being present and creating a harmonious home, maybe by cooking, maybe by suggesting things to do, helps James and the girls function better when we are all together.

A simple act, like being present, or mentioning something you think they are doing "right" is often useful to the other person.

I like this exercise because it trains us in detachment from outcome while at the same time engaging our mental energy to come up with useful details that help.

What are ten things you could do?

1 _____

2 _____

3 _____

4 _____

5 _____

6 _____

7 _____

8 _____

9 _____

10 _____

☐ PHYSICAL   ☐ SPIRITUAL   ☐ EMOTIONAL

124) Suggestions To The Wealthiest People In the World

$\backsim$

Here is the scenario. In four hours you are going to give a talk, you will have the ears of the most powerful and rich people in the planet, and they are all willing to hear your ideas.

What are your ten ideas and why should they spend money on them?

I would suggest investing money in educating (teaching how to write and read as well as creating small businesses) to women all over the world who live in war zones or in countries where men oppress them.

There are charities that do it, but if I had the most powerful and rich people listening in I would suggest creating task forces to recruit local women and through any means possible so that they get the benefits.

WHAT ARE TEN IDEAS *you give to these powerful and wealthy people?*

1 _____

2 _____

3 _____

4 _____

5 _____

6 _____

7 _____

8 _____

9 _____

10 _____

❑ **PHYSICAL**   ❑ **SPIRITUAL**   ❑ **EMOTIONAL**

125) What Are Ten Services You Wish
Amazon Could Do For You?

I get lots of shopping done through Amazon, not just books but also bulk groceries and even household items.

I wish they had an hourly delivery. I think they are working on that, but it is still my idea. I also wish I could rent fancy clothes, say for example, designer clothes through Zappos, which is owned by Amazon.

I also wish they had fresh produce delivery... That is a wish that is hard to fulfill, but this is just ideas.

The more you do the better. And remember that if you feel they have energy, just go ahead and send them.

WHAT ARE YOUR TEN IDEAS *for the supermarket*
of the world, otherwise known as Amazon? Tweet me
@ClaudiaYoga #IdeaMachineAmazon

1 _____

2 _____

3 _____

4 _____

5 _____

6 _____

7 _____

8 _____

9 _____

10 _____

☐ PHYSICAL ☐ SPIRITUAL ☐ EMOTIONAL

126) Ten Things You Can Learn In 10 Minutes
That Add Value To Your Life

I found this question in Quora and loved browsing through the thousands of answers. Feel free if you want to do that as well.

One answer I found in Quora, was something my grand father told my father and then my father told me. Papalino, my grandfather, suggested you never pull a little piece of skin when it is sticking out because you will keep on pulling and hurt yourself. Instead, take a nail cutter and cut the piece at the root so it does not stick out any more.

This piece of advice continues to surprise me for how true and effective it is.

What are your ten ideas?

1 _____

2 _____

3 _____

4 _____

5 _____

6 _____

7 _____

8 _____

9 _____

10 _____

☐ PHYSICAL   ☐ SPIRITUAL   ☐ EMOTIONAL

127) What Would You Say Are The Top 10 Moral Underlying Stands You Live By and Why?

W̶e all have an inner compass, and we all live by some rules, either imposed or clearly thought out, or somewhere in the middle.

Identifying them makes us more self aware and clearer in our actions. And how we act, the example we give is much more of a teacher than anything we say.

For me, not lying while being kind is a daily underlying theme. Sometimes it is hard, but I try to keep it in mind as a practice.

What are ten that you live by?

1 _____

2 _____

3 _____

4 _____

5 _____

6 _____

7 _____

8 _____

9 _____

10 _____

☐ PHYSICAL   ☐ SPIRITUAL   ☐ EMOTIONAL

128) TOP TEN
CREATIVITY TIPS

Y ou are about to face an audience of writers, musicians, dancers, filmmakers and artists of all kinds.

You are required to offer ten valuable tips for creativity.

Think of what artists go through, sometimes they get stuck, sometimes they get no inspiration, sometimes they are down.

How can they deal with these ups and downs?

I find that the number one tip for creativity is to do something, whatever it is you are working on, daily. The daily practice is the sweating carpet on which the muse can fly and inspire us whenever she is ready.

WHAT ARE YOUR TOP TEN CREATIVITY TIPS?

1 _____

2 _____

3 _____

4 _____

5 _____

6 _____

7 _____

8 _____

9 _____

10 _____

☐ PHYSICAL ☐ SPIRITUAL ☐ EMOTIONAL

129) Write 10 Things You Are Grateful For
When It Comes To Your Parents

⌐⌐

No matter weather your parents are alive or not, if they lived with you while growing up or not, or whatever your circumstances may have been. There is always a reason to be happy, for example, at a simple level, we are alive, we are functional and we are exercising our minds. That is thanks to them, no matter what or where they are.

Many people, me included, carry some emotional baggage regarding parents, but finding gratitude for them is always helpful in letting go and also, in realizing that they did the best they could and that they tried hard, even though it may or may not have looked that way.

What are ten things *you can be grateful for*
when it comes to your parents?

1 _____

2 _____

3 _____

4 _____

5 _____

6 _____

7 _____

8 _____

9 _____

10 _____

☐ **PHYSICAL**   ☐ **SPIRITUAL**   ☐ **EMOTIONAL**

130) Write A Letter to The 80-Year Old You. Tell Him or Her Ten Things You Are Doing Today To Help the Future You.

A t 80 I hope to be able and healthy, as much as possible. So in my letter I would write to her that I am trying to eat little carbs and avoid inflammation, I am doing yoga to keep flexible and listing ideas to keep the mind sharp.

What are the ten things *you can write to your 80 year old you?*

1 _____

2 _____

3 _____

4 _____

5 _____

6 _____

7 _____

8 _____

9 _____

10 _____

☐ PHYSICAL   ☐ SPIRITUAL   ☐ EMOTIONAL

131) 10 SMALL GIFTS I
COULD GIVE TODAY

The other day I noticed that in the studio where we record podcasts they had run out of green tea with lemon grass.

Someone in the kitchen said: "everyone seems to like it". I thought that it could be a good idea to send some. And I did. It is not a great big present; it is more like a gesture.

As you go through the day see if there are any details, any little thing that could make someone smile.

WHAT COULD BE TEN LITTLE PRESENTS?

And note that they do not have to be expensive.

1 _____

2 _____

3 _____

4 _____

5 _____

6 _____

7 _____

8 _____

9 _____

10 _____

☐ PHYSICAL   ☐ SPIRITUAL   ☐ EMOTIONAL

132) 10 People I know I could ask a question whose answer would help others

~~

My brother has been working on the radio for over 25 years. He is now a teacher at Buenos Aires' Instituto Superior de Enseñanza Radiofónica.

If I could ask him a couple of questions on producing shows I am pretty sure he would add value to others. I could ask him for example what are the three most important things to consider when designing a new show, or podcast.

Who are ten people you know *that are experts at something and what could you ask them to add value to others?*

1 _____

2 _____

3 _____

4 _____

5 _____

6 _____

7 _____

8 _____

9 _____

10 _____

☐ PHYSICAL   ☐ SPIRITUAL   ☐ EMOTIONAL

133) 10 Books everyone under 25 MUST READ AND WHY?

This is a matter of opinion of course. We all have books that have resonated with us. For example, who can forget the concept of the 10,000 hours introduced by Malcom Gladwell, or the concept of the Pareto Law? I personally like books that talk about deep personal experiences and in turn teach something, like for example Oriah Mountain Dreamers's *The Invitation*.

A more recent book I would recommend is *Choose Yourself*, because the world we live in has changed so dramatically in such out of proportion ways that I feel it is important to be informed and have new strategies for coping in the new landscape.

What are the ten *you would recommend and why?*

1 _____

2 _____

3 _____

4 _____

5 _____

6 _____

7 _____

8 _____

9 _____

10 _____

☐ PHYSICAL   ☐ SPIRITUAL   ☐ EMOTIONAL

134) Ten Ways I Can Give Something Other Than Money

I read recently that homeless people in New York feel unseen. People avoid looking at them.

I feel that way too sometimes, and even though saying that I can relate to homeless people would be inappropriate as I have food and shelter, being seen is one of the most important human needs we all have.

Giving can be as simple as really being present for my step-daughters and noticing how beautiful they are, and telling them. Or meaning it when I say thank you to a stranger for holding the door open for me.

What are ten other ways *you could give today?*

1 _____

2 _____

3 _____

4 _____

5 _____

6 _____

7 _____

8 _____

9 _____

10 _____

☐ PHYSICAL   ☐ SPIRITUAL   ☐ EMOTIONAL

135) 10 GREAT REMINDERS EVERYONE COULD KEEP THROUGHOUT THE DAY

W hen I was growing up I saw the serenity prayer hanging in my grandparents house. I had no idea of what was going on there as they lived really far and I seldom saw them, but the words hanging on the wall had an impact on me, they left me considering what they meant and they seemed very wise.

In Twitter I usually send yoga-related tweets and the ones with most engagement have to do with reminders to "relax the face, relax the neck, and breathe". So much so that I think having a reminder somewhere on the wall that says "relax the face" could be useful.

WHAT WOULD YOU INCLUDE *in your ten reminders to hang on the wall?*

1 _____

2 _____

3 _____

4 _____

5 _____

6 _____

7 _____

8 _____

9 _____

10 _____

☐ PHYSICAL   ☐ SPIRITUAL   ☐ EMOTIONAL

136) IDENTIFY SOMEONE YOU ADMIRE AND WRITE TEN IDEAS FOR HIM OR HER

I admire Dave Asprey for his book *The Bulletproof Diet* that has recently been released. He has done a ton of research and some of the suggestions in his book have been working for me.

Ever since reading about him I have been thinking about bulletproof exercises, meaning the minimum viable exercises one could do to bulletproof the body and maintain a regular sense of health. These would probably include yoga exercises, especially the five most important ones that include: forward bends, back bends, hip openers, twists and inversions. I may be writing that as a blog post soon.

When we interviewed Dave, James suggested he write a bulletproof for creativity. Dave thought it was a great idea and who knows? Maybe if you Google it today it may exist as a post or a book.

WHAT ARE TEN IDEAS *for someone you admire?*

1 _____

2 _____

3 _____

4 _____

5 _____

6 _____

7 _____

8 _____

9 _____

10 _____

❏ Physical   ❏ Spiritual   ❏ Emotional

137) 10 Places Where I Could Show Up More

⌒

Life has gotten busy for me ever since I started writing ten ideas a day. Just the listing of ideas gives me enough fire to come up with a new creative adventure every so often and as a result life keeps moving and changing.

One area that has fallen through the cracks a bit is my closet. As I look at the state o fit I notice it is not as orderly as it once was.

I would like to show up a little more in the area of de-cluttering in my life because I believe when I have less things then I have more space, not just to be, but also to think, and to create.

What are your ten?

1 _____

2 _____

3 _____

4 _____

5 _____

6 _____

7 _____

8 _____

9 _____

10 _____

☐ PHYSICAL   ☐ SPIRITUAL   ☐ EMOTIONAL

138) 10 Wise Sayings You Can Remember And Why?

My favorite saying is attributed to the Buddha. Apparently he said: "Don't believe a word I say". I like it because he had zero need to prove anything, and if anyone wanted to they could just go ahead and try and see if it worked for them.

Of course there is a funny line doing the rounds that goes: "I don't remember ever saying that", which is also attributed to the Buddha. In the end who knows what he said or did not say?

What are ten sayings *you like, and remember, and why?*

1 _____

2 _____

3 _____

4 _____

5 _____

6 _____

7 _____

8 _____

9 _____

10 _____

❑ PHYSICAL   ❑ SPIRITUAL   ❑ EMOTIONAL

139) 10 Bumper Stickers You Can Create or Can Remember and Why?

I used to have one that read: "honk if you don't exist". I got it at a meditation retreat up in Colorado, and it caused lots of interesting distractions as I drove through New Jersey for a couple of years.

What are ten bumper stickers
you like or you think should exist and why?

1 _____

2 _____

3 _____

4 _____

5 _____

6 _____

7 _____

8 _____

9 _____

10 _____

☐ PHYSICAL   ☐ SPIRITUAL   ☐ EMOTIONAL

140) You Just Took The Red Pill. You Wake Up. What are 10 Ways In Which you are Different?

⸻

The red pill is the one that shows reality as it is. Once you take it that's it, things get real; life is very different than before.

One thing that I guess would be immediately apparent to me is that I need to pull my own weight, do my work, show up every day, and not rely so heavily on others.

What are ten things *that become apparent to you after the red pill takes effect?*

1 _____

2 _____

3 _____

4 _____

5 _____

6 _____

7 _____

8 _____

9 _____

10 _____

☐ PHYSICAL   ☐ SPIRITUAL   ☐ EMOTIONAL

141) 10 Ways To Organize Finances and Why Are They Worth Doing?

⌐═

Finance issues cause back pain, and they bring in a lot of anxiety. Generating ideas everyday is one way to come up with new ways of creating opportunities for abundance, but the issue remains, how can we organize our finances?

One thing that has helped me, when I do it, which I have not done in a couple of months, (my bad!) is to go over the expenses of the month.

I keep an Excel spreadsheet so that business and personal expenses can be identified and separated.

It feels good when I do it. Another idea could be creating a budget, which is useful for many people.

WHAT ARE TEN IDEAS *on how to organize your finances and why are they worth doing?*

1 _____

2 _____

3 _____

4 _____

5 _____

6 _____

7 _____

8 _____

9 _____

10 _____

☐ PHYSICAL   ☐ SPIRITUAL   ☐ EMOTIONAL

142) TEN SMALL BUSINESSES THAT COULD THRIVE IN YOUR NEIGHBORHOOD

L ook around the area where you live. Have you ever needed something and not been able to find it?

The small town where I live in has many resources but it lacks a good supermarket. The organic section of the one we have tends to have old, sorry looking vegetables.

Of course because of the Hudson Valley during the summer there are lots of farmer markets, but I find during the winter months we could definitely use some good veggies, and a good supermarket would provide that.

WHAT ARE TEN THINGS *needed in your neighborhood?*

1 _____

2 _____

3 _____

4 _____

5 _____

6 _____

7 _____

8 _____

9 _____

10 _____

❏ PHYSICAL   ❏ SPIRITUAL   ❏ EMOTIONAL

143) IDENTIFY TEN PROBLEMS AND COME UP WITH A SOLUTION

❝ Don't create a business", said one of the sharks from the TV show *Shark Tank* while speaking to an audience of military entrepreneurs in the White House. "Identify a problem and solve it", he said, "the business will come second".

I hate the cold. That is my problem. I wish there was a jacket that *stopped* the cold, and was cozy, amenable, soft, and light in weight, and also, not very expensive.

There. One problem. One solution.

WHAT ARE YOUR TEN?

1 _____

2 _____

3 _____

4 _____

5 _____

6 _____

7 _____

8 _____

9 _____

10 _____

❏ PHYSICAL   ❏ SPIRITUAL   ❏ EMOTIONAL

144) TEN WAYS TO MAKE MONEY WITH YOUR CAR

I once went to a meditation retreat in the mountains of Colorado and met a woman who told me she was living on her car. Later that day I had a chance to look at such car, it was filled with books, pillows, and garbage bags filled with clothes. It looked pretty dirty.

But what if someone could figure out a way to live on a car and do it right? Think about it! They could create a 40-page booklet about it and sell it, which would give this exercise an "idea sex" flavor. Other ideas could be to rent it, or to go shopping for people... the possibilities are endless.

WHAT ARE YOUR TEN WAYS *of making money with your car?*

1 _____

2 _____

3 _____

4 _____

5 _____

6 _____

7 _____

8 _____

9 _____

10 _____

☐ PHYSICAL   ☐ SPIRITUAL   ☐ EMOTIONAL

145) 10 Suggestions To Stop A
Mind Gone Wild

Sometimes my mind takes over and goes into a loop. It is impossible to stop it. I've tried many things, like meditation, breathing, etc. Nothing seems to work.

One thing that helps me is to have a dialogue with it and invite it, since it is in override mode anyways, to come up with ideas. But it seems to give me a lot of resistance to that suggestion.

Once the mind is gone into crazy mode it is hard to reel it back. But that should not stop us from coming up with ideas of what we could try to do, for whenever it might happen again.

What are your ten suggestions?

1 _____

2 _____

3 _____

4 _____

5 _____

6 _____

7 _____

8 _____

9 _____

10 _____

☐ PHYSICAL ☐ SPIRITUAL ☐ EMOTIONAL

146) WHAT ARE THE TEN TRAITS THAT MAKE A GOOD TEACHER?

A great teacher is someone that will say something that on the surface seems innocent, a passing remark, and yet leave me thinking about it for weeks.

It's like when Tony Robbins' teacher said to him: "this is the next move", when an anxious Robbins wanted to move things along and onto the next move that would lead him towards a black belt. The teacher brought him back to the present, and to the subtle difference that made his repetition number 300 different than his repetition number 299.

Great teachers have the ability to knock us off our socks with one well-crafted observation, one inspiring challenge, or one word of advice that changes our whole outlook.

WHAT ARE TEN QUALITIES *you can think of?*

1 _____

2 _____

3 _____

4 _____

5 _____

6 _____

7 _____

8 _____

9 _____

10 _____

☐ PHYSICAL   ☐ SPIRITUAL   ☐ EMOTIONAL

147) TEN SUGGESTIONS TO
DEAL WITH DEBT

There are many college students graduating with debt these days. Looking back, when I was in debt, I wish someone had told me earlier to get a hold of my finances and make plans to pay little by little.

Becoming debt-free took me years.

IF YOU WERE TALKING TO A RECENT GRADUATE *with,*
say, 100,000 in debt, what would be your ten suggestions to become debt free?
Note that your suggestions can include reading literature, or watching films.
Get creative with your idea machine.

1 _____

2 _____

3 _____

4 _____

5 _____

6 _____

7 _____

8 _____

9 _____

10 _____

☐ PHYSICAL ☐ SPIRITUAL ☐ EMOTIONAL

148) Ten Classes You Took In Your Life
That You Liked and Why

~~

I remember one of my first yoga classes back in 1999 at Equinox. The instructor's name was Michael, and that is all I know.

I really liked Michael's class back then because through the practice he pointed my attention towards muscles I was not aware I had.

What are ten classes *that you enjoyed in the past and why?*

1 _____

2 _____

3 _____

4 _____

5 _____

6 _____

7 _____

8 _____

9 _____

10 _____

❏ PHYSICAL   ❏ SPIRITUAL   ❏ EMOTIONAL

149) Ten Suggestions For Themes That Other People Could Write Ideas On To Help Themselves

⌒

Yes I am asking you to do exactly what I am doing. Come up with ten suggestions for people to come up with ideas that will help them.

As an example you can use any of the first 90 suggestions in this book, which were all "themes" targeted towards helping yourself.

What are the ten themes *that others could use?*

1 _____

2 _____

3 _____

4 _____

5 _____

6 _____

7 _____

8 _____

9 _____

10 _____

☐ PHYSICAL   ☐ SPIRITUAL   ☐ EMOTIONAL

150) Ten Themes Suggestions For Ideas
Other People Could Write
to help others

Now move it one step further *and come up with 10 themes for other people to come up with ten ideas that can help others.*

1 _____

2 _____

3 _____

4 _____

5 _____

6 _____

7 _____

8 _____

9 _____

10 _____

☐ PHYSICAL   ☐ SPIRITUAL   ☐ EMOTIONAL

151) How Can I Monetize My Website, or Podcast?

~~

Recently someone submitted a question for Ask Altucher. This person had a website that specialized in tiny houses.

I love the idea of tiny houses; I think they are cute, inexpensive, and sustainable. I like that they set people free financially, but I wonder if I would be able to live with James in a space that is less than 200 square feet and do yoga and write together.

But I digress. This person said that his podcast/internet page had about ten thousand committed followers/listeners and he needed help monetizing.

One idea I had was to have a course, i.e.: a video course on how to transition from living in a normal size house to living in a small space, including all the psychological drama that could go along downsizing to such an extreme level.

People who may love tiny houses as I do, *but fear the experience, could be potential buyers of a course like that which could be an up sale for the free content. What are other ten ideas you would suggest?*

1 _____

2 _____

3 _____

4 _____

5 _____

6 _____

7 _____

8 _____

9 _____

10 _____

❑ Physical ❑ Spiritual ❑ Emotional

152)MAKING A BORING PROFESSION INTERESTING: TEN IDEAS

S omeone needs your help. She works in a profession she considers "boring" like law, or medicine. She wants to write about it and make interesting but fears it will not attract readers. After all who wants to read about a new code or regulation.

However, I am pretty sure I would read an article that told me the ten new laws that just passed and how they affect me, especially if it was broken state by state.

For example, I am pretty sure nobody understands the repercussions of the new health-care laws. Any lawyer that makes it simple, tells a story, and writes it well, would have my attention.

SO LET'S HELP THIS PERSON, *how can they make their topic more interesting? Take the law, or medicine; what ten articles would you want to read from the experts?*

1 _____

2 _____

3 _____

4 _____

5 _____

6 _____

7 _____

8 _____

9 _____

10 _____

❑ PHYSICAL   ❑ SPIRITUAL   ❑ EMOTIONAL

153) Ten Ways To Improve Writing

W e are listing ideas here, but many of them can easily sprout into posts, articles, and even books.

But good writing takes skill. Many disagree on the best ways of writing but in the end it comes down to a practice. And practice requires showing up, and tuning up our skills.

One tip that I find dreadful but tremendously useful is to show up for the page every day. I don't like it because on some days I don't feel like it, but then again, that is what a practice is.

Showing up creates the sacred space of sorts, where we are able to exercise the muscles needed, so when the muse is ready to send us a good idea we are prepared, all the pencils are sharp, the blank page is ready to receive and we can download the great story, or post, or idea that is coming through us.

What are ten ways *to improve writing?*

1 _____

2 _____

3 _____

4 _____

5 _____

6 _____

7 _____

8 _____

9 _____

10 _____

☐ PHYSICAL   ☐ SPIRITUAL   ☐ EMOTIONAL

154) TEN TIPS FOR
PUBLIC SPEAKING

Tell me your suggestions on how to prepare for a talk I need to give tomorrow. There is no time for research and no time to look at books or see videos on YouTube, so you need to come up with clear and specific guidelines. What can one do to prepare?

Since I am the one giving the talk, in this made-up scenario, let me clarify that I know the topic inside out and I even have an outline. What I need are suggestions on the actual speaking in public. For example, opening up with a joke, if it is a good one, can be a good idea. Remembering to breathe is important.

WHAT ARE TEN SUGGESTIONS *you can come up with to help me? Tweet to me the good ones @ClaudiaYoga #IdeaMachineTalkTips*

1

2

3

4

5

6 _____

7 _____

8 _____

9 _____

10 _____

◻ PHYSICAL   ◻ SPIRITUAL   ◻ EMOTIONAL

155) TEN SURE WAYS TO DESTROY YOUR RELATIONSHIP

W e may not all know exactly how relationships work, there are just so many variables that is next to impossible to give a list that applies to everyone. But I know that if I don't watch certain things I can turn my own relationships into disasters of tears, angry discussions and wounded souls.

We have all been that gal or that guy who just does not get it.

For example: I find that a breach of trust is a sure way to destroy a relationship. Going behind someone's back breaks any sense of safety. It works like poison. I learned that lesson early on, when I was very young, and it still holds because it is extremely important.

Knowing where we go wrong is helpful so that we can avoid mistakes in the future. And sharing our mistakes with others can point the way so others do not make those mistakes or at least consider them.

WHAT ARE YOUR TEN IDEAS ON THIS?

1 _____

2 _____

3 _____

4 _____

5 _____

6 _____

7 _____

8 _____

9 _____

10 _____

☐ PHYSICAL   ☐ SPIRITUAL   ☐ EMOTIONAL

156) TEN SUPER FOODS YOU LOVE THAT EVERYONE SHOULD TRY

⌒⌒

I've tried so many different diets and foods that I am exhausted I know that refined sugar and flour are the enemies of my system, which does not mean I avoid them completely, as I still like French toasts once in a while, but I do try to stay clear of them, as much as possible.

Steaming vegetables and adding good fats (like good quality olive oil) has been a blessing. I've read about it in countless books but I know they work because I've tried them in my system. Steaming avoids burning the nutrition and putting the oil at the last minute helps keep the good fats alive (rather than burning them). So for example, steamed cauliflower, blended with a bit of grass-feed butter and good quality salt, makes for a delicious *mash* that has no potatoes in it, and James likes it too, which makes it a double winner at home.

WHAT ARE YOUR TEN SUPER FOODS, *as you define them, meaning foods you know work for you?*

1 _____

2 _____

3 _____

4 _____

5 _____

6 _____

7 _____

8 _____

9 _____

10 _____

❑ PHYSICAL   ❑ SPIRITUAL   ❑ EMOTIONAL

157) Ten Life Tips
You Can Offer

~~

O ne thing I've learned is to NOT respond to haters on the Internet. If I do not engage, within 24 hours I am clear of the metallic taste and discomfort. If I do, and try to defend myself, then the cycle restarts, because a hater will never say: "oh you are right", no, they will always keep on pushing buttons when they know that one is alive and feed on the cycle of destruction.

WHAT ARE TEN LIFE TIPS *you can offer?*

1 _____

2 _____

3 _____

4 _____

5 _____

6 _____

7 _____

8 _____

9 _____

10 _____

☐ PHYSICAL ☐ SPIRITUAL ☐ EMOTIONAL

158) Ten Trends You See Coming
In The Next Century

O ne trend I see exploding is the sharing of things.

For example: Have a car but no job? Sign up with UberX and drive people around while getting paid for it… Have a home but will be away? Share it through AirBnb.

Whenever I travel I much prefer to rent a house where I can cook my own meals rather than be confined to a small hotel room with food that I never know how is prepared.

So that is one trend I see expanding, the sharing of everything.

WHAT ARE OTHER TRENDS YOU SEE? *List ten:*

1 _____

2 _____

3 _____

4 _____

5 _____

6 _____

7 _____

8 _____

9 _____

10 _____

❑ PHYSICAL   ❑ SPIRITUAL   ❑ EMOTIONAL

159) IDEA SEX TEN INVENTIONS FOR THE TEN TRENDS

Y esterday you listed ten trends. Now, let's come up with ten ideas for these industries.

For my idea of the sharing economy, I would like to be able to rent everything, from a yoga mat that is delivered to wherever I am staying (by someone who signs up to UberYoga and is in the neighborhood) to bicycles, to boats, to ping-pong tables, and on and on.

WHAT ARE YOUR TEN IDEAS?

1 _____

2 _____

3 _____

4 _____

5 _____

6 _____

7
_____

8
_____

9
_____

10
_____

☐ PHYSICAL   ☐ SPIRITUAL   ☐ EMOTIONAL

160) Ten Car Games For People Driving With Children

~~~

It does not matter if you already know the games or if you are coming up with them, as long as you come up with ten.

In a long car ride from Austin to San Francisco a friend of mine once pointed out all the cars that had plates that read something interesting, like "DAGIRL" or "THEONE" or… you know? Those kinds of license plates.

As a game, granted, it won't last long but it makes for a pastime and can distract children, even if for a few minutes.

What are other ten ideas *you can come up with to help over-stressed parents driving little ones in the back?*

1 _____

2 _____

3 _____

4 _____

5 _____

6 _____

7 _____

8 _____

9 _____

10 _____

❑ PHYSICAL   ❑ SPIRITUAL   ❑ EMOTIONAL

161) 10 Suggestions For Car Rental Companies

You probably rented a car already, or maybe you used Zipcar? Or maybe Car-2-Go. All of them are attempting the same, the share economy for cars, and they are pretty good at it, but they could be a lot better.

If you've never had to rent a car, imagine landing, tired, in a new city, and having to go to another terminal, with your luggage and signing contracts! A thing of the remote past in our days of online transactions and apps that can do it all.

However, this is how many of the rental companies operate, they have to get you to verify things, sign up for insurance at the counter etc. It is very messy.

One proposal I have is an app on which I can upload everything, including my driver's license and credit card. They'd also know my preference of insurance and, guess what? Since they are already on my phone they would know when my next JetBlue fight is happening, which could have companies competing for my business (sending me offers).

Then when I land all I would have to do is get a map to where my car is. That's it. No showing anything, no talking to anybody, and the closer to my landing terminal the better.

What are your ten ideas?

1 _____

2 _____

3 _____

4 _____

5 _____

6 _____

7 _____

8 _____

9 _____

10 _____

❑ PHYSICAL   ❑ SPIRITUAL   ❑ EMOTIONAL

162) What Should Uber Do Next: 10 Suggestions

⌒

Uber is probably the up-and-coming trillion dollar company of the near future. And that is because their strength is not just in being a cab-driving company but rather on the infrastructure they will have to provide services that include delivery and errands.

If you have not heard of Uber yet, then you should, because it is likely we will hear a lot more about them and they just closed a funding round at a 40 billion dollar valuation which makes them huge.

My first idea for them would be that I could ask for dry cleaning and super-market pick-ups.

What are ten suggestions *you can come up with?*

1 _____

2 _____

3 _____

4 _____

5 _____

6 _____

7 _____

8 _____

9 _____

10 _____

❏ PHYSICAL   ❏ SPIRITUAL   ❏ EMOTIONAL

163) 10 Decisions You've Made
Without Thinking Much

W̶e all make decisions that affect our lives without thinking at some point or another because we are humans and that is the nature of the beast, we do not have all the information, or we get confused, or we have some preconditioned ideas and we just… well, make a mistake.

Not thinking things through can be expensive. For example: when I bought a home in the suburbs of New Jersey where I would live by myself for five years, I never, in a million years, anticipated, nor was I told, about the infinite number of repairs and re-carpeting, and toilette fixing, and pipes breaking, and trees that become a liability to the town because they are sick.

I never imagined I would spend so many weekends working on a house that was so tiny. For all of the first three years I never left the house. All my money and life-energy went into this property, I had nothing left for me, and I barely had money for food.

If I had known this, it would have helped me make a more educated decision. That decision probably would have been to not buy a house because I am terrible at repairing roofs, leaks and building up walls from scratch or painting walls, fixing showers, et all.

WHAT ARE TEN DECISIONS *you made without thinking that impacted you and that you could tell others about?*

1 _____

2 _____

3 _____

4 _____

5 _____

6 _____

7 _____

8 _____

9 _____

10 _____

☐ PHYSICAL   ☐ SPIRITUAL   ☐ EMOTIONAL

164) Ten Things You Bought In the Past Six Months, And Why?

Look back and think of products you bought in the past six months. Sometimes we make educated purchases and buy things we really need and that help us, sometimes we are not so lucky.

In this case I would like to focus on things that you bought consciously which you use and that are helping you, and why is that. For example, I heard about a crow funding project that is raising money for smart earplugs. These ear-plugs have the noise cancellation effect I like (I love silence) and also connect to my phone for music via blue tooth. Not only that but they are also ergonomic and not bulky, a plus if I want to use them for sleep.

I am waiting for the delivery and it won't happen until May of 2015, so I have a ways to go, but I am happy with the investment because having silence helps me enormously with productivity and also with meditation, with going within and quieting the senses and the nervous system.

What are ten conscious purchases
you made in the past six months and why?

1 _____

2 _____

3 _____

4 _____

5 _____

6 _____

7 _____

8 _____

9 _____

10 _____

☐ PHYSICAL   ☐ SPIRITUAL   ☐ EMOTIONAL

165) Alternatives To Getting An Expensive College Education

College cost is at an all time high and the level of debt of recent graduates is alarming. For many of the younger generations it might not make sense to pay such enormous amounts of money and make that kind of a key decision at an age (18) when not many of us know exactly what we would be getting into.

My suggestion is travel, because leaving money and arguments, after 12 years of sitting in front of a slide deck of teachers it might be a very good idea to go and see what the real world is all about before going for 4 or 8 more years of more sitting and listening to people who may or may not own a passport.

WHAT ARE TEN SUGGESTIONS *you could give as alternatives to someone considering skipping college?*

1

2

3

4

5

6 _____

7 _____

8 _____

9 _____

10 _____

☐ PHYSICAL   ☐ SPIRITUAL   ☐ EMOTIONAL

166) Ten Things To Consider Before Renting (or Buying) Your Next Home

O n average people move every five years, so why not put a bit of attention into this and make a nice list that can help others move with more awareness.

One idea I have is to temporary rent a place in the neighborhood to see how things go. Anyone can do this through Airbnb which rents places for two or three days. That way one could get much more of a feel for a neighborhood than if, say, visiting for just the showing of an apartment or house.

If budget does not permit, then I would spend some time in the neighborhood anyways, and I would check for potential freeway noise, or airport noise, or wildlife noise (once we rented a place that had a family of alpha ducks living in the backyard and they were loud), and so on.

Another thing worth considering is weather the type of stores you like are in the area, or libraries, or movie theaters.

What are the ten *considerations you would list?*

1 _____

2 _____

3 _____

4 _____

5 _____

6 _____

7 _____

8 _____

9 _____

10 _____

☐ PHYSICAL   ☐ SPIRITUAL   ☐ EMOTIONAL

167) Ten Things You'd Want To Say To Your Great Grand Daughter When She Is 10 Years Old.

Suppose you have a pregnant 15-year old daughter now. Okay, that is not a pretty image, perhaps it is too scary, but for the sake of argument, let's pretend it happened and you are happy about it.

Let's say she has a child when she turns 30, that would be your grand-daughter, and this child, in turn has a child at 30, that would be your great grand-daughter. So 2015+15+30+30+10= the year is now 2100.

One thing I'd like to tell this ten-year-old is that there is great wisdom in sitting in silence. To remember that as she ages. That a lot of good ideas come from letting go, from just being rather than always doing.

To recap: It's the year 2100 and you have a 10-year-old great grand-daughter.

You are not on the planet anymore *but there is a letter for her with ten things you want her to know. She opens it, what are the ten things she reads?*

1 _____

2 _____

3 _____

4 _____

5 _____

6 _____

7 _____

8 _____

9 _____

10 _____

❑ PHYSICAL   ❑ SPIRITUAL   ❑ EMOTIONAL

168) TEN MOST INFLUENTIAL PEOPLE OF THIS DECADE AND WHY?

To me, having strong women in positions of power is a great thing because it encourages more of us to share our wisdom without fearing, without giving in to the voices that go deep into our psychic telling us to be "nice" instead of to take risks and do what we know we love doing.

I find Sheryl Sandberg, the COO of Facebook, to be such an influencer of our times. I like that her book, *Lean In*, reopened a conversation that is worth having. For example, in her book I learned that women tend to raise their hands and ask questions a lot less than men, say, during conferences or lectures. I then noticed this when I myself offered workshops or talks.

Needless to say I now ask questions every time even if I think my question may not be so smart. If I want to know something, or if I need to clarify a point, then I raise my hand. Thank you Sheryl.

WHO ARE YOUR TOP TEN AND WHY?

1 _____

2 _____

3 _____

4 _____

5 _____

6 _____

7 _____

8 _____

9 _____

10 _____

☐ PHYSICAL   ☐ SPIRITUAL   ☐ EMOTIONAL

169) Ten Alternatives to The End-Of-The-Year 'Gift Crazy'

I hate the consumerism powered by guilt and triggered by commercials around holidays.

I prefer to do gifts of memories and experiences instead of things. Not those those are free, but at least they can be more thoughtful, more planned out, and have more meaning.

This is my opinion, so for me, an alternative would be that whatever we feel like giving, and it does not have to be anything (I am fine with no presents) has to be hand-made, so that a memory of craft and giving is created rather than an just act of consuming.

What are your ten *alternatives and why?*

1 _____

2 _____

3 _____

4 _____

5 _____

6 _____

7 _____

8 _____

9 _____

10 _____

☐ PHYSICAL   ☐ SPIRITUAL   ☐ EMOTIONAL

170) TEN THINGS THAT EVERYONE
SHOULD UNCLUTTER

A rtificial plants. Who came up with this idea? It seems to me it's just made-in-china plastic posing for life.

I think this is one thing that every household should recycle responsibly into something else, or in plain terms, get rid off.

WHAT ARE, IN YOUR OBSERVATIONS, *ten things that we should all get rid off and why?*

1 _____

2 _____

3 _____

4 _____

5 _____

6 _____

7 _____

8 _____

9 _____

10 _____

☐ PHYSICAL ☐ SPIRITUAL ☐ EMOTIONAL

171) Ten Keeping
It Real Cards

⌒⌒

C ome up with ten lines for hallmark cards that keep it real. For example: I
am out of here, for when you want to quit. Short, quick and to the point.

What are your lines *and why are they keeping it real?*

1 _____

2 _____

3 _____

4 _____

5 _____

6 _____

7 _____

8 _____

9

10

☐ PHYSICAL   ☐ SPIRITUAL   ☐ EMOTIONAL

172) TEN THINGS I FEAR LOSING AS I AGE

W e all face death and with it we encounter all kinds of possibilities for difficult gratitude problems. For example: loss of friends, loss of sight, mobility, sometimes sickness and the dreadful death of loved ones.

Of the things that go when we grow old, what are ten you are afraid to let go of? For me it has to be the people I love, that is my number one fear.

In doing this exercise I am reminded both that I can't hold them forever, but at the same time, I can be kind to them today.

WHAT ARE THE TEN THINGS *you fear losing and what do they point to?*

1 _____

2 _____

3 _____

4 _____

5 _____

6 _____

7 _____

8 _____

9 _____

10 _____

❏ Physical   ❏ Spiritual   ❏ Emotional

173) TEN QUESTIONS WE SHOULD ASK OF OURSELVES MORE OFTEN

WHO AM I?

I keep thinking I am what I write, what I eat, whom I am with, my body, my possessions, my story. Is that really true?

All wise traditions point to the fallacy of that answer to the question. Further they suggest the answer cannot even come from the mind.

So this is one of those questions I ask myself often. Another one is: "Do I want peace or do I want this?" That one helps me get out of trouble again and again because it re-focuses me into what is important.

WHAT ARE TEN YOU WOULD SUGGEST?

1 _____

2 _____

3 _____

4 _____

5 _____

6 _____

7 _____

8 _____

9 _____

10 _____

☐ PHYSICAL ☐ SPIRITUAL ☐ EMOTIONAL

174) If you Had To Start All Over Again, What Would Be 10 Things You Would List Today?

~~~

S ay you have no food, no clothes, no relationships, nothing. You are stripped to nothing, you are homeless.

Welcome to the worst possible case scenario.

What are ten things you could do, from this place, to start rebuilding?

I would make it a priority to find shelter first, of course, and food. I would not stop until that, but I would make sure, along the way, to take some time to be quiet.

I would make them go hand-in-hand. Perhaps as I do even today. Hunting for food, sitting in silence.

Because it is in silence that I get *downloads* as of what the next step is for me.

I would not be surprised if some of us avoid this list, but an idea machine would never shine away from it.

What are your ten?

1 _____

2 _____

3 _____

4 _____

5 _____

6 _____

7 _____

8 _____

9 _____

10 _____

☐ PHYSICAL   ☐ SPIRITUAL   ☐ EMOTIONAL

175) 10 Ideas You Would Be Afraid To Give Away For Free, Because They Are Very Valuable

T hink of one organization, or one person that you KNOW you can help. For example, it could be someone from whom you just attended a workshop or whose books you've read, and then plan ten ways in which they could really be helped.

The challenge today is not so much to come with the ten but to make sure that the ten are so good that the receiver would want to use them, with or without you.

Then you can think about giving them away for free… no attachments. At day 175 your Idea Muscle fitness is in top shape, you are an idea machine; there is no more fear, other than what may be left on your head. This is why this list comes now.

What are those ten amazing ideas?

1 _____

2 _____

3 _____

4 _____

5 _____

6 _____

7 _____

8 _____

9 _____

10 _____

❏ PHYSICAL   ❏ SPIRITUAL   ❏ EMOTIONAL

176) THE 10 MOST POWERFUL EMOTIONS AND HOW YOU'VE COPED WITH THEM IN THE PAST

A nger comes to mind immediately. Perhaps because of the harsh sentiment it carries and its brutal ability to destroy everything on its way.

Anger is one I try to ease from, and stay away from. I handle it from many different angles, because I find that no one-thing works with it. It is sneaky, and it is unpredictable. God knows what creak in my psychic will be triggered by a smell, a word, or a turn in the events that lead to the sale of my now deceased father.

So I deal with it by walking, by doing yoga, by being aware of when it overtakes me and removing myself from the situation until when I can cool down. I deal with it by sitting in silence and feeling it in full, even though I hate feeling it, I just seat with it, observing the feelings, without attaching any new story lines to the emotion.

WHAT ARE THE TEN *you can identify and how can you deal with them?*

1 _____

2 _____

3 _____

4 _____

5 _____

6 _____

7 _____

8 _____

9 _____

10 _____

◼ PHYSICAL ◼ SPIRITUAL ◼ EMOTIONAL

177) 10 Ancient Recipes You Know That Heal Common Pains

M y grandmother used to place her feet on hot water before going to bed. She slept well.

I don't know how much that works, but I do know that taking chamomile tea before sleep helps me. Or even better, there is a type of tea you can get in the supermarket called "sleepy time", and this one gets me into the zone and ready for sleep fast.

WHAT ARE TEN THINGS *you know to work for common issues?*

1 _____

2 _____

3 _____

4 _____

5 _____

6 _____

7 _____

8 _____

9 _____

10 _____

◻ Physical   ◻ Spiritual   ◻ Emotional

178) 10 Words That Should Come Out Of Our Vocabularies For The Benefit Of All

❝ *It's your fault"* or anything that produces blame is one sentence I would like to see eradicated. If only so that we could take enough time to realize our part in the dance of wrong-doing, because blaming always includes two people, and where there are two individuals there are also two versions.

Finding fault in others keeps us small and blind to the fact that as humans we need to take responsibility for how we act, what we do, how we affect the lives of others. Even if we perceive ourselves as completely blame-free.

What are ten words *or phrases you would eradicate,*
or suggest we eradicate, and why?

1 _____

2 _____

3 _____

4 _____

5 _____

6 _____

7 _____

8 _____

9 _____

10 _____

☐ PHYSICAL   ☐ SPIRITUAL   ☐ EMOTIONAL

179) TEN WAYS I AM DIFFERENT AS AN IDEA MACHINE

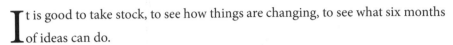

It is good to take stock, to see how things are changing, to see what six months of ideas can do.

For me, listing the ideas has resulted in a sharp, trained brain, in coming up with suggestions I did not now I had spontaneously while in meetings, and in being more careful when it comes to when I speak and why I do so.

I've also come across certain books that I felt I had to read, and in reading I found more inspiration.

As I finish this book I would like to hear from your experience, especially if you are finishing it with me and you have 179 lists in your hand. Tweet me any insights @ClaudiaYoga #IdeaMachineDay179.

WHAT ARE YOUR TEN WAYS *in which you are different because of listing ideas daily?*

1 _____

2 _____

3 _____

4 _____

5 _____

6 _____

7 _____

8 _____

9 _____

10 _____

❑ PHYSICAL   ❑ SPIRITUAL   ❑ EMOTIONAL

180) Ten Words Of Wisdom From You To Anyone Who May Be Thinking Of Trying This Idea Machine

O ne thing I would say to anyone reading is to not believe what anyone says and rather try it.

It is not my line; I stole it from the Buddha whom I think is the first and best marketer in the history of humankind because 'don't believe a word I say' is the best copy-writing line I've ever read.

But beyond taking ideas from enlightened people, I would say that this coming up with ideas has not been easy.

However, showing up offers a payoff. It's like they say about musicians, if they don't practice one day they notice, if they don't practice for two days then the conductor notices, and if they don't practice for three, then the audience notices…

It applies here as well. I can tell when I don't exercise my idea muscle one day. If two days go by then James notices, and if more days go by, well I don't have a huge audience judging me as I don't play an instrument in a theater, but I am sure everyone would notice.

What are the ten words of wisdom
from you to someone considering trying?

1 _____

2 _____

3 _____

4 _____

5 _____

6 _____

7 _____

8 _____

9 _____

10 _____

☐ Physical   ☐ Spiritual   ☐ Emotional

BONUS LIST #DEEP

I propose you list 10 things you would like someone to read about you on the day you are buried or the day in which our ashes are spread over whatever body of water.

As I ponder over what the list would contain for me, very quickly I see the possibilities for wisdom and deep ignorance, or both.

With that very simple idea for a list: "come up with 10 things you wish people say when you die", we are faced with legacy, with how we want to be remembered, what are the important things that we notice in our lives, and also the places where we miss the mark a bit.

Do I want to be remembered for some high achievement? Do I want to day-dream of how James would say something like: "*she was a brave soul that crossed continents in search of her dreams and the call from spirit*" or do I want specific words, a foundation that donates X moneys, the eradication of a disease, words that meant things to people.

As I sit here on a chill morning under the rumbling sound of planes on their final descend onto Fort Lauderdale, this is what comes up:

I want to be remembered as a woman who was not especially talented per say but who tried hard. Someone who faced enormous disruptions early on and through leaving them behind both in body and mind ended up in new countries.

And right there I can tell my ego is playing a game. It does not even want to show its true colors, because it is being watched. And saying that I am not so special is a form of reverse ego, it is like fishing for the "c'mon, yes you were" and then the smile. I want to look good on paper.

But a list it is, so let's list:

- A CITIZEN OF THE WORLD. No country was ever home because home was wherever she was

- A PROFOUND YOGA TEACHER who searched far and wide for whatever truly worked

- A WRITER that made a contribution through sharing stories

- A CANTADORA, keeper of the tradition of story telling, I borrowed this one from Clarissa Pinkola Estés because I like the sound of that word in Spanish

- AN EMOTIONAL WRECK of an individual who plunged deep into her own psychic to face her inner demons and tried to arrive at some wisdom.

- A FEARLESS SEEKER of truth

- A WOMAN LIVING IN A TIME when womanhood began to awaken

These come to mind now. They are all-noble and let's face it, a bit aggrandizing, they make me feel good, and they point to things that are important to me today.

Here is what I gather from the eulogy:

James is important to me, as well as the children in my life, the space in which I am now, regardless of location. Truth is important to me. Writing through what inspires me, in the hope of helping others sometimes, but aware that this is not my job. I don't get to decide who helps whom.

At the moment of this writing I am 46. That means there is probably less amount of life going forward than there was before. Values, ideas and sensations change. Noticing my own mortality points to what is real with more clarity.

Nothing I *have* will come with me as I cross into the formless state, nothing I claim to be mine, or even to love will make the transition onto the other side by my side, not even James.

It is sobering to remember that what is of real value has no monetary tag attached to it.

In the end I am but a swift inhalation and exhalation, with a huge amount of drama in between. This life I so cherish is brief and passing and I cannot even control what will be said in my eulogy, not to mention how long it will be remembered for.

Nobody cares.

The older I get not even I care about the set of ideas I think to be me.

And so, in the eulogy, perhaps I would like something for me too. I would like to have something that cannot be said or understood, something that only I can get, which is freedom.

I'd like it to be noted, not for the listeners but for the silent absence of my mind at that time, that I was able to stop the insanity of wanting to please, from wanting to control outcomes, from trying to control, gain, or outsmart time, freedom from space and from to get glimpses into what it means to be truly, fully now.

And that is not a list point I'm afraid. It is just a letting go, a realization of the preciousness of this very moment, in each moment, all the way to the point where everything is really gone and that eulogy is enunciated by a voice, or not – it doesn't matter.

For you however, it may be different. Perhaps you have a lot more life to look forward to in the future than what you have lived. In that case this list is also helpful in pointing to what is really important to you.

Because when it's 9 AM and we needed to be in the car by 8:45 and we are late, that we focus on what is important, so that we do not waste any more time.

And that's how it is when we face death, we get really clear on what is important, and surprisingly enough it may not be the money, or the new job, or the book we wanted to write. It might turn that what is important has to do with our relationships to those we love deeply, and maybe even a softening towards our own self.

It might turn out that we can relax a bit more into just being rather than doing. It might be that we can give ourselves a break.

I have done my ten ideas for the day. Now is time to stand at the edge of the yoga mat.

ABOUT

THE AUTHOR

C LAUDIA AZULA ALTUCHER is a writer, podcast host, speaker and teacher of yoga. She is the *WSJ* bestselling co-author of *The Power Of No*, and author of *21 Things To Know Before Starting An Ashtanga Yoga Practice*.

She writes for national media outlets including Thought Catalog, Mantra Yoga + Health, and Positively Positive.

410

She is the host of The Yoga Podcast and co-host of the Ask Altucher Show.

Her blog ClaudiaYoga.com has attracted 2.5+ million visits since inception. You can find her on Twitter @ClaudiaYoga or listen to her show at TheYogaPodcast.com.

Claudia would like to hear from you, she answers direct questions on AskClaudiaYoga.com

CLAUDIA AZULA ALTUCHER

WSJ BESTSELLING CO-AUTHOR OF *THE POWER OF NO*

ISBN-13:978-1502593009 • ISBN-10:1502593009